Praise for *The Socialist Temptation*

"*The Socialist Temptation* explains the inexplicable: Why have so many people over so many generations come to believe that a government monopoly of power and control will improve life? Why has repeated failure not dissuaded them? Freedom—real political and economic freedom—delivers all that socialism has promised but never delivered over the centuries. *The Socialist Temptation* explains why so many painfully refuse to learn."
> —**Grover Norquist,** founding president of Americans for Tax Reform

"Socialism does not come offering bread lines, secret police, or gulags. It sells itself as a decent and uplifting creed. It appeals to our belief in fairness, in kindness, in standing up for the little guy—even, sometimes, in patriotism. Iain Murray takes those claims seriously. Instead of using socialism as a swear word, as conservatives sometimes do, he properly analyzes its appeal. When a lot of people, even on the right, are falling for arguments that ought to have been discredited long ago, this is a vital task— especially so, perhaps, during the authoritarian spasm that has followed the coronavirus infections. Restoring freedom is going to be a grueling and arduous task. Here is the instruction manual."
> —**Daniel Hannan,** former Member of the European Parliament and founding president of the Initiative for Free Trade

"Several volumes could be written about the failures of socialism, but Murray has artfully condensed the argument to two hundred pages."
> —**Daniel Mitchell,** president of the Center for Freedom and Prosperity

"America needs this book! *The Socialist Temptation* provides a reasoned and sympathetic critique of socialism that appeals to values that most Americans hold, whether they identify as left, right, or center. I would have liked to write a book like this if I hadn't spent my time drinking in commie countries."
> —**Benjamin Powell**, co-author of *Socialism Sucks: Two Economists Drink Their Way Through the Unfree World*

"Why is Karl Marx more popular than Frédéric Bastiat? Because Marx promised people something for nothing, while Bastiat explained that 'something for nothing' is a scam. In *The Socialist Temptation*, Iain Murray explains why the scam is making a comeback, and why it is still a scam."
> —**Glenn Reynolds**, Beauchamp Brogan Distinguished Professor of Law at the University of Tennessee and founder of InstaPundit

"Iain Murray has written a book that is horrifyingly essential. Socialism was a backward idea in the nineteenth century and a catastrophe in the twentieth, and yet it somehow limps on among the worst sort of political cretins in the twenty-first. As Murray shows, socialism's promises of justice and liberation are a lie and always have been. It is a philosophy of domination and brutality—it always has been and always will be. It is our good fortune that Iain Murray is around to write this book—and our tragedy that we need him to."
> —**Kevin Williamson**, reporter, columnist, and author of *The Politically Incorrect Guide to Socialism* and *The Smallest Minority*

"Iain Murray's *The Socialist Temptation* is a much-needed reminder of the tragic toll that socialist and interventionist policies have taken on the lives of the very people they claim to help."

 —**John Berlau,** senior fellow at the Competitive Enterprise Institute and author of *George Washington, Entrepreneur*

"Iain Murray's *The Socialist Temptation* is just the current of fresh water needed to transform 'the swamp.' Twenty years of poor economic policy from both Democrats and Republicans have caused the American economy to stagnate. The punk growth rate caused the U.S. economy to be vastly poorer ($20T instead of $30T) than what free markets could have generated for all of us to enjoy. What to do? Populist 'conservatives,' whom Murray astutely calls out, are tempting us with socialist remedies dressed up in red, white, and blue bunting. They, along with left-wing 'reformers' like Elizabeth Warren, do not understand that *you cannot drain a swamp*. (A founding owner and manager of The Dismal Swamp Company, George Washington almost went broke trying in 1763.) The one and only solution is to flood the fetid swamp with the fresh waters only free enterprise can provide, turning it into a vibrant, thriving, life-filled wetlands. The sweet intellectual waters of Iain Murray's *The Socialist Temptation* to the rescue!"

 —**Ralph Benko,** chairman of The Capitalist League and co-author of *The Capitalist Manifesto*

"With the rise of belief in socialism among young people, we need a book about it that they'll read. This is it. Iain Murray has written a masterpiece of concise evidence-based argument

that demolishes socialism in every particular. It's short. It's highly
readable. And it packs an intellectual punch."

    —**John O'Sullivan,** president of the Danube Institute
       and author of *The President, the Pope, and the Prime
       Minister*

THE SOCIALIST TEMPTATION

THE SOCIALIST TEMPTATION

IAIN MURRAY

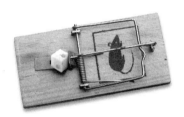

REGNERY GATEWAY

Regnery Gateway™ is a trademark of Salem Communications Holding Corporation
Regnery® is a registered trademark of Salem Communications Holding Corporation

ISBN 978-1-68451-060-3
eISBN 978-1-68451-075-7

Library of Congress Control Number: 2020932586

Published in the United States by
Regnery Gateway
An imprint of Regnery Publishing
A Division of Salem Media Group
300 New Jersey Ave NW
Washington, DC 20001
www.Regnery.com

Manufactured in the United States of America

10 9 8 7 6 5 4 3 2 1

Books are available in quantity for promotional or premium use. For information on discounts and terms, please visit our website: www.Regnery.com.

For Fred Smith

CONTENTS

Foreword

BY ŽILVINAS ŠILĖNAS
PRESIDENT, FOUNDATION FOR ECONOMIC EDUCATION

W hen I watch the videos of crowds of cheering Lithuanians toppling statues of Lenin in every city, town, and village in the 1990s, I am filled with both joy and regret.

I rejoice that the Berlin Wall, the Soviet Union, and its physical artifacts have been destroyed. It brings a smile to my face to know that countless statues of Communist dictators have been torn down and sold for scrap. I take glee in the fact that an aluminum bust of Lenin is now a can of Coca-Cola or a car.

Because neither Coke nor cars were available to us living in the Soviet Union. Of course Pepsi opened a plant in the USSR in 1974, and in the late eighties the Soviet Union exchanged warships for syrup, but that's a story for a different time.

It's not as if the Soviet Union lacked resources to produce cars or cans. After all Russia's natural resources were (and still are) vast. In the minds of central planners, who view the economy as a function of natural resources, Soviet citizens should have lived in material abundance. But in reality everyone wallowed somewhere close to poverty—especially by today's standards.

I don't think anyone starved to death in the Soviet bloc in the late 1980s, but there was a constant shortage of things that people liked— from meat to mayonnaise to canned green peas to toilet paper. Which is especially telling of socialist central planning, because it is not difficult to produce toilet paper.

Shortages in the Soviet Union are not really news—although watching the "Democratic Socialists," I begin to doubt that. What may be less known is that even when consumer goods were available, their cost was astounding. Imagine spending the equivalent of four months' pay for a TV, two months' pay for a refrigerator, or two weeks' pay for a raincoat! Americans pay five to ten times less for a much better model. These were the actual prices for consumer goods, if you were lucky enough to get them.

And you needed luck. For things like color TVs you had to wait for a year or so to get the right to buy it. Or you could win a right to buy a TV at a trade union raffle (that's how we got ours). The queue to buy a Soviet automobile, which was an inferior knock-off, was seven years or more.

Don't think that "Ladas" were cheap and that queues were a way to ration super affordable automobiles to the masses at below-market prices. You were expected to fork out at least five years of wages for it. That's like paying supercar prices for a clunker without air conditioning!

No doubt someone will accuse me of being a materialist who is ignoring the spiritual aspects of living in the socialist system. I have two things to say. First, you would not find a less spiritual system than Soviet socialism. Unless you count blind obedience to the Communist Party a spiritual faith.

Second, only in a society with material abundance can you live a life without caring about material goods. It is precisely when material goods are in short supply that they become essential status symbols.

Only in a country devoid of material goods does a colorful Western-made tracksuit signal that you are better than your fellow men.

Critics of Western consumerism employ logic reminiscent of Schrodinger's Cat. On the one hand they accuse Westerners of obsessing over things; on the other they lament that Westerners do not value consumer goods enough. There was no such ambivalence behind the Iron Curtain! If you want to see a society obsessed with things, try socialism, where shopping for shoes is similar to a hunt, and successful purchase of a pair of the right size is like meeting your spirit animal.

In case you wonder why I mentioned the "right size," a smart tactic was to buy shoes even if they didn't fit you with the hope of trading them for something different. When the choice is between shoes of the wrong size and no shoes, the choice is rather simple.

Mind you, these are recollections from the 1980s, the era of "Perestroika" and "Glasnost." I am not talking about purges, collectivization, deportation, gulags, and forced famines. I am not talking about multiple environmental disasters, the absence of any human rights, criminal charges for homosexuality, or countless other horrors that every person with integrity should abhor.

Moreover, most of these travesties were not unfortunate side-effects or unintended consequences of the pursuit of the greater good. Collectivization—the confiscation of the private property of peasants and landowners; forcing them into collective farms; shooting, starving or deporting the people who resisted—was absolutely intentional.

Collectivization was necessary to implement the Communist dictum that the means of production should belong to the state. So, no, the "but it wasn't real socialism" evasion that the left in the West is so keen to employ when confronted with the reality of the Soviet Union has zero credibility. Environmental devastation was a result of poor planning, hubris, not really caring, or a price worth paying in the minds of central planners.

Remember the last episode of Chernobyl, the trial scene when the prosecutor asks why the design of the nuclear reactor was shoddy? "For the same reason our reactors do not have containment buildings around them, like those in the West. For the same reason we don't use properly enriched fuel in our cores. For the same reason we are the only nation that builds water-cooled, graphite-moderated reactors with a positive void coefficient. It's cheaper."

On May the 1st, 1986, my family skipped the Mayday parade and went sunbathing at a nearby lake, for it was unusually warm. The lake stank of industrial runoff from a nearby leather factory, but I guess it was more enjoyable than carrying red flags and screaming praises of the Communist Party. Chernobyl had exploded on April 26 of that same year, and the radioactive clouds were travelling westwards right across Lithuania. But no one told us.

I could go on for hours (maybe I am getting old),but let me say it once more: I rejoice that the Soviet Union is dead, I rejoice that the peoples of Eastern Europe had a chance to choose their own paths. I am ecstatic that they chose capitalism. Trust someone who has lived in both systems. The further from socialism—whether in years or in kilometers—the better.

Now comes the regret.

It comes from the feeling that the celebrations, although warranted, were premature. We destroyed the facade of socialism, but we have not eradicated the virus. Imagine a scientist who could have eradicated the plague, but didn't, and now sees the resurgence of a new viral strain. Or think of Isildur, who could have tossed the ring into Mount Doom after defeating Sauron at the end of the Second Age. Or of the German soldier in *Saving Private Ryan* who is spared and released only to rejoin his comrades, continue the fight, and mock the American soldier who spared him.

Nazi Germany underwent extensive denazification to make sure National Socialism was eradicated. Somehow regular socialism escaped that fate, adapted to new surroundings, and resurged.

As with any virus worthy of its name, socialism has mutated, evolved to survive in the changed environment, and continues to poison our lives. True viruses hijack the cells of the body and force them to spread the virus further. In a similar manner, institutions intended to serve society have started replicating and spreading socialist ideas. Some schools now prioritize ideology over pursuit of knowledge. In some media, truth is replaced with "social justice." Some treat self-reliance and personal responsibility like artifacts of a bygone era, mocked by politicians on stage who are performing a farce by the name of "More Free Stuff."

So there we are. Hungover from the victory over socialism in the 1990s, feeling that the victory is slipping away, shocked with disbelief that Sanderses and Corbyns are relevant in the countries of Reagan and Thatcher. Unsure what to make of woke-ness, the Green New Deal, and young people's support for all sorts of socialist ideas. Feeling like the old man at the end of *Cabaret* as the crowds join the young blond in Hitlerjugend uniform singing "Tomorrow Belongs to Me."

Are we winning this battle? Well, we have not lost yet. Now is certainly not the time to head for the hills or to barricade ourselves in ideological fallout shelters to wait out the apocalypse.

We must reach the rising generation with the ideas we know allow individuals to build prosperity and self-realization. We must speak in terms people understand; we have to demonstrate how free markets and free societies solve the problems that people care about. It is our job to show that free markets work better than any oppressive economic system. We must be bold, smart, sincere, and uncompromising on the core issues of liberty and free markets. Or at least those of us for whom defense of liberty is a spiritual calling, professional fulfillment, and a 24/7 job. I know it is for me, I know it is for Iain.

Thank you, Iain, for this book.

Trigger Warning

This book may offend you.

◆

It points out that many of the ideas currently popular among self-described democratic socialists are dangerous.

◆

Socialism is dangerous for working people.

◆

It's dangerous for racial minorities.

◆

It's dangerous for women.

◆

Implementing socialism has resulted in millions of deaths—even when that looked unlikely at the start.

◆

And that was real socialism.

◆

If this offends you... you've probably stopped reading this book already.

◆

For the rest of you, who are open to the idea that socialism might be a temptation America cannot afford, read on.

PART ONE

Socialism: A Myth That Refuses to Die

CHAPTER 1

A Twenty-First-Century Buzzword

Socialism is tempting, seductive, alluring. It comes in many forms and speaks in many different vocabularies. It appeals to people who value fairness, who value freedom, and who value security. It comes in many varieties, sometimes clothing itself in the dress of nationalism, sometimes in the garb of environmentalism. Yet there is one single, unifying feature shared by every version of socialism: subjugation of the individual to the collective.

While Americans have always been skeptical of socialism, even in the Progressive and New Deal eras, that is beginning to change. Large numbers of Americans now express admiration for socialism, and similar numbers are critical of the free enterprise system. The problem is particularly acute among America's young people.

Almost 50 percent of Millennial and Generation Z respondents told the Harris Poll in February that they would prefer living in a socialist country. In June, over half of all women aged eighteen to fifty-four polled by the same organization said the same thing.

Socialist policies enjoy even more widespread support than socialism under that name. Huge numbers of Americans support universal healthcare, free college education, or "a living wage."

Legislators and presidential candidates are now packaging these policies together in proposals like the "Green New Deal," which enjoy widespread public support.

Even conservatives are beginning to espouse socialist economic policies. Tucker Carlson has praised Elizabeth Warren's "economic patriotism." Many conservatives advocate breaking up big businesses and regulating them harshly. Support for redistributive policies such as wage subsidies and "industrial policy" is growing in places left behind by the economic recovery since the great recession. Capitalism is in crisis as socialism rides high.

This is not the first time we have been here. In 1977, when America was deep in an economic malaise, Ronald Reagan, at that time the governor of California, gave a speech at Hillsdale College in which he asked, "Whatever happened to free enterprise?" Noting that the free enterprise system "for 200 years made us the light of the world," Reagan warned that freedom is "never more than one generation away from extinction." He took the lead in preserving it for the previous generation. It is time for this generation to take up the torch.

Yet saying that we need to defend American liberty against socialism raises the question: What exactly is the "socialism" that people say they approve of? Is the word actually meaningful at all?

To some extent it isn't. Socialism has become a bit of a buzzword. To many progressives, describing something as socialist is now simply a sign of approval. To many conservatives, describing something as socialist is a sign of disapproval. If socialism is just a political label, it probably isn't anything to worry about.

Perhaps socialism is just a fad. Or even a social media phenomenon. We live in an era when a freshman congressman can become one of the most recognizable political figures by means of an outspoken Twitter account. On July 1, 2018, Alexandria Ocasio-Cortez told

NBC's *Meet the Press* that while socialism is "part of what I am; it's not all of what I am," going on to say, "[I]t's not about selling an '-ism' or an ideology or a label or a color. This is about selling our values."[1] If that's the case, perhaps socialism is just a marketing gimmick.

Yet beneath the rhetoric, there is something profoundly worrying here. To understand the very real danger, we need to look at what people have generally meant when they talk about socialism—and exactly what it is about that that appeals to Americans today. To help, we can look at the previous times when America has flirted with socialism.

Americans are an idealistic people. When our ideals seem to align with policies that have proven themselves harmful time and again, that's when bad things start to happen.

So we need to worry not just about the ideology that goes under the name socialism, but also about socialist policies under any other name. Distressingly, Americans today may be even more enthusiastic about socialist policies than they are about socialism under that label. While they remain somewhat wary of the ideology, the policies align with their values.

CHAPTER 2

What Is This Socialism Thing, Anyway?

Socialism comes in many guises. It'll behoove us to discuss as many of them as possible before we go on. Trying to define socialism can be like trying to nail jello to the wall. People who are proud to call themselves socialists under one definition would recoil in horror at being tied to another definition. Sometimes a socialist, particularly a politician, will say he follows one definition of socialism while at the same time advocating policies that belong to a different strand. Some politicians advocate socialist policies while denying being socialists at all. Below are a few of the seemingly infinite varieties of the creed.

Marxism: While Karl Marx may not have been the first socialist (a variety of liberal and utopian thinkers could lay claim to that title), he and Friedrich Engels were the first to develop a complete theory of socialism. Marxists believe in a class struggle between the capitalist bourgeoisie and the proletariat working class, who are exploited so that they do not receive the full value of their labor. The remedy is a revolution of the proletariat against their exploiters, leading to the workers' control of the means of production, distribution, and exchange. This is the classical kind of socialism that led to revolutions in Russia and China and their transitions to communism.

Communism: This is the state of affairs after the revolution, as in the Soviet Union and its satellites, with the state controlling industry and directing the economy through a system of command and control by public officials, who are members of the Communist Party. Democracy is subsumed to the will of the Party but given nominal preeminence. Elections are for show, as are trials. The dead giveaway that a country is communist is that it calls itself a Democratic People's Republic. Communism is now mostly extinct.

Democratic Socialism: This can be thought of as Marxism without revolution. The supposed problem (the capitalist exploitation of workers) and ultimate remedy (the workers' control of factories and the like) are the same. But that remedy is achieved not by violent revolution but by means of democratic elections. This was historically the approach of Western European socialist parties such as Britain's Labour Party, which after winning the election of 1948 proceeded to nationalize vast areas of British industry. This system was dismantled by Prime Minister Margaret Thatcher in the 1980s. And consistent defeat at the ballot box led the Labour Party to abandon its support for public ownership and turn to "social democracy" under Prime Minister Tony Blair.

Social Democracy: This is a European variant—usually a mixed economy with a highly regulated private industry and an extensive welfare state paid for by high tax rates to correct the wrongs of capitalist exploitation. Today most Western European countries practice some form of social democracy. The mixed economy garners support from conservative and Christian Democrat parties for social democracy in those countries.

Note that social democracies can enjoy more freedoms in certain areas than America, such as Sweden's system of school choice.

As Kristian Niemietz of London's Institute of Economic Affairs puts it, the difference between social democracy and socialism is "the difference between a large state and an interventionist state. The Nordic economies are characterized by high taxes and high levels of public spending, but they are otherwise relatively liberal market economies."[1]

Market Socialism: Recognizing the importance of markets and prices in efficient resource allocation—something that we'll discuss later—some socialist countries have moved from public ownership and command-and-control direction of industry to worker-owned cooperatives. The former Yugoslavia, Cuba to some degree, and countries as diverse as Belarus and Ethiopia have adopted elements of market socialism in an attempt to keep their socialist systems going. In some cases, businesses may be run by the state, but profits are distributed to citizens. The Alaska Permanent Fund can be thought of as a market socialist enterprise.

State Capitalism: The Chinese system of "socialism with Chinese characteristics" is an example of state capitalism: there is a large degree of market freedom, but there is no doubt about who is in charge, and that isn't the People—as we saw when the NBA and its stars kowtowed to the Chinese government over the question of the Hong Kong protests. Institutions such as the Chinese Communist Party and the People's Liberation Army have special roles in company charters or ownership, and property rights are weak. State capitalism bears a strong relationship to fascism.

Fascism: While any socialist worth his or her salt will vigorously deny that fascism is a variant of socialism (and we should always remember that the Nazis persecuted Marxists), the parallels are clear. Mussolini combined socialism with nationalism to create his "third way." Modern socialists condemn fascism as friendly to capitalism, but the truth is that fascism subsumed private industry beneath multiple layers of state control and planning. Competition was replaced by state-organized cartels, small companies were dissolved, and corporations were instructed to act in the national interest—as defined by the ruling fascists. As Sheldon Richman puts it in *The Concise Encyclopedia of Economics*, "Planning boards set product lines, production levels, prices, wages, working conditions, and the size of firms. Licensing was ubiquitous; no economic activity could be undertaken without government permission. Levels of consumption were dictated by the state, and 'excess' incomes had to be surrendered as taxes or 'loans.'"[2] All this was supposedly for the benefit of the society. The similarities between fascism and socialism are so great that the Austrian economist Ludwig von Mises found the difference only a "trivial technicality."[3]

Radical Environmentalism: Socialism has taken on a new form with the emergence of Green parties in Europe. In this telling of the tale, it is not just the working class that is exploited but the environment itself. Capitalism must be constrained more to "save the planet" than to empower the worker. Some industries must be shut down and all individual lifestyles constrained to protect the environment, even if the poor, as well as the rich, suffer from the constraints. But the tools by which this is done are to large extent Marxist in nature. Groups such as Extinction Rebellion have even adopted the rhetoric and some of the actual tactics of revolution.

Clearly, socialism comes in many varieties. It is not uncommon to find two different forms of socialists arguing over the true meaning of the term. In fact, the history of the international socialist movement (particularly its Trotskyite wing) is one of repeated schisms over small matters of principle. This phenomenon was memorably satirized in Monty Python's *Life of Brian*, where the People's Front of Judea expressed more contempt for the Judean People's Front than for the Roman occupiers.

There is one unifying factor, however, shared by all varieties of socialism: they subjugate the individual to the collective. This goes from working for the state under Marxism to having large amounts of your property taken away under social democracy to being thrown in prison for dissent under fascism or state capitalism. Two corollaries arise from this fact.

First is the need for bureaucracy. While modern socialists may claim that they believe in decentralization and local control, they also agree that there is a need for strong regulation to prevent things like pollution. Regulation requires regulators. Regulators need to be experts. These two immutable factors lead inexorably to bureaucracy.

All socialist states need bureaucrats, as a 1929 British General Election poster for the Conservative Party pointed out. It read, "Socialism would need inspectors all around," and depicted six officious-looking men in peaked caps eyeing "an Englishman's home," as the horrified occupant looked on. Anyone who has tangled with the Environmental Protection Agency (EPA) when trying to build on his own land would appreciate that.

The other corollary is expropriation. While many modern socialists do not believe in the wholesale abolition of private property, all socialist states require some level of redistribution of wealth. Generally, the state's take comes directly out of your paycheck, so you never even see all the income you earned, except as numbers on a paystub. In benevolent Sweden, for example, the tax rate on incomes above about $70,000 is 69.8 percent (including about 10 percent nominally paid by the employer).[4] When Britain was a democratic socialist country in the 1960s, the socialist prime minister Harold Wilson introduced a 95 percent "supertax" on the rich, which led to pop superstars The Beatles releasing their song *Taxman* in protest.

So to sum up, a simple but comprehensive definition of a socialist regime is one in which the individual is subject to control by the collective, to the determinations of bureaucrats, and to the expropriation of wealth. How such a dreary situation could continue to be attractive is the true mystery—and the subject of this book.

One final note here: part of the temptation of socialism is that its message of exploitation and class struggle can be dressed up in other clothes. The socialist may claim exploitation and demand redistribution of wealth to bring down the powerful—when what's really going on is that people who have reached a position of wealth and power in business are using laws and regulations to prevent others from competing with them. What is actually needed is deregulation to allow for competition, but the temptation is to go for the socialist policy, which inevitably leaves everyone worse off.

Religion teaches us that injustice is to be recognized and corrected. Faith leaders of all denominations decry inequity and exploitation from the pulpit. When the cry is "something must be done," socialism provides a ready answer for what that something should be. Thus socialism becomes attractive to those whose faith calls them to act.

This leads to the paradox of our times: even some avowed conservatives espouse socialist policies. This is particularly true of conservatives who identify conservatism with populism or nationalism. Populist conservatives tend to see successful capitalists, at worst, as traitors to "the national interest," or at least as indifferent to their fellow citizens. Thus they find the purported remedies offered by socialism attractive, even if they don't call themselves socialists. But if it walks like a duck and quacks like a duck, it's a duck. Socialism adopted in "the national interest" is going to come with all the same problems as socialism adopted to promote the international brotherhood of the worker. Policies that impose bureaucratic controls and redistribute wealth are socialism in fact, no matter what they're called.

CHAPTER 3

Socialism in American History

While socialism under that name has rarely been a big thing in American politics, we've seen plenty of periods when socialist policies have been popular. In most of those cases, the socialism has been described in nationalist terms, characterized as something that sets America apart from other less enlightened nations. There were two large waves of socialism in American history: the Progressive Era and the New Deal.

In the 1890s, Marx was a mere footnote in history. While his dream was of a revolution by an educated working class, it was the middle class that was the driving force the first time America was tempted by socialism. Inspired by concern over pollution, political corruption, "Robber Barons," immigration, and alcoholism, the middle class was the driving force in pushing America towards Progressivism.

Progressivism has all the hallmarks of socialism—starting with collectivism. The Progressives blamed "individualism" for many of the ills Progressivism was supposed to solve. The concept of "association," a sort of solidarity alliance between the classes, was proposed instead. The "Upper Ten" (the "upper ten thousand" residents of New

York City, that is) became the subjects of hatred, much like the One Percent after our own recent financial crisis. Labor unions grew in power, with questions surrounding labor and employment leading to the creation of a U.S. Department of Labor.

Bureaucracy was the main weapon for bringing the "individualists" to heel. In 1887 the Interstate Commerce Commission was founded to regulate railroad shipping rates. In 1914 it was used as the model for the Federal Trade Commission, founded to bust trusts and rein in the Robber Barons. Meanwhile the U.S. Department of Agriculture started inspecting food manufacture and also formed a Bureau of Chemistry that would later become the Food and Drug Administration. President Woodrow Wilson championed the creation of the Federal Reserve, bringing central banking back to the United States.

Expropriation was also a focus. After an 1895 loss at the Supreme Court, supporters of a national income tax managed to pass the Sixteenth Amendment between 1909 and 1913, enabling Wilson to switch the income base of the nation from tariffs to income tax. The mechanism for much future expropriation had been secured.

The Progressives were also concerned with the perfectibility of man. By 1918, every child in America was required to complete elementary school, and an education bureaucracy was a priority of Progressives at the state and local levels. The Progressives introduced eugenics into America to lower the numbers of the poor, the disabled, and the immoral. They passed the Eighteenth Amendment to prohibit making, transporting, and selling alcoholic beverages. They restricted immigration and used public schooling to Americanize immigrants' children.

Labor unions were very influential in the Progressive movement, but they did not become a vehicle for an outright socialist political movement as they did elsewhere in the developed world at the time—at least partly thanks to Samuel Gompers, who was the president of the American Federation of Labor (the forerunner of the AFL-CIO) from 1886 until his death in 1924.

Gompers was familiar with Marxism but rejected the idea of revolution, preferring instead that workers should put their faith "into purely industrial or economical class organizations with less hours and more wages for their motto." His emphasis was on the workers, not the class, and so he helped to exclude unskilled workers from the union movement. The result was a less political labor movement in America than in other countries. While labor disputes were frequent and often violent, they were disputes over the conditions of workers, not class war.

While the Progressive era was socialist as broadly defined, it was not Marxist. Thus it set the pattern for America's long-running on-again, off-again affair with socialism.

◆   ◆   ◆

Most Americans think the New Deal happened because Herbert Hoover turned the Crash of 1929 into the Great Depression by pursuing a "laissez-faire" approach to the economy. Hoover was indeed to blame, but for very different reasons. Hoover's reaction to the great crash was to embark on a series of socialist-lite interventionist policies that made things worse, laying the groundwork for the New Deal to keep doing more of the same.

In what he called "the most gigantic program of economic defense and counterattack ever evolved in the history of the Republic," Hoover took the wrong position on practically everything. Treasury Secretary Andrew Mellon advised him to "liquidate labor, liquidate stocks, liquidate the farmers, liquidate real estate. Purge the rottenness out of the system. High costs of living and high living will come down. ... enterprising people will pick up the wrecks from less competent people"—advice that was harsh, but fair.[1] Mellon would probably have been proved right.

Instead, Hoover went down the path of government intervention. He created a bailout program, the Reconstruction Finance Corporation, to prop up failing banks, businesses, and local governments; he increased federal spending; his Emergency Relief and Construction Act aimed to cure unemployment and provide funds to businesses through a program of public works; he inserted the federal government into the mortgage industry with the Federal Home Loan Bank Act; and he agreed to the disastrous Smoot–Hawley tariffs, which most economists today believe significantly prolonged the Depression.

He also proved friendly to the labor movement, signing the Davis–Bacon Act, which instituted "prevailing wages" for public works projects (vastly increasing their cost even today), and the Norris–LaGuardia Act that significantly strengthened labor unions and put employers at a disadvantage.

And in 1932, Hoover signed the largest peacetime tax increase in American history.

Does any of this sound like "laissez-faire" to you?

Of course, none of it worked. The gross national product dropped 30 percent during Hoover's presidency. His opponent, New York Governor Franklin D. Roosevelt, was able to blame Hoover for the Depression and to argue that even more interventionist policies would be the way to get out of the slump. Progressive commentators of the time excoriated Hoover not just for his failure, but for being of the wrong class—a member of an old order that needed to be swept away.

After assuming the presidency, FDR doubled down on everything Hoover had done and then some. His program to reform the

American economy was vast and sweeping. It represented not just a revolution for the American economy but a political realignment that lasted into the 1960s.

The hallmark of the New Deal was the subjugation of the individual to an extent that had proven impossible even for the progressives. Throughout the Progressive Era, the Supreme Court had stood up for the individual's freedom to contract with others. This is known as the Court's Lochner Era, named after a 1905 case ruling that state limits on working hours were a violation of the individual's freedom of contract.[2] Because, according to the Supreme Court, freedom of contract emanated from the Due Process clause of the Constitution, this interpretation is often called "substantive due process."

Thus all sorts of laws and regulation that are accepted today were viewed by the Court as unconstitutional. For the New Deal to work, that had to change. After the court had struck down a series of attempts to impose regulations and restrict freedom of contract, President FDR proposed a law that would have allowed him to pack the Court with his appointees (ostensibly to ease the workload on aging justices).

In a case called *West Coast Hotel Co. v. Parrish*, which concerned an attempt to impose a minimum wage for women, Justice Owen Roberts, who had previously sided with the conservative justices known as "the Four Horsemen of the Apocalypse" performed what became known as the "switch in time that saved nine," and voted for the constitutionality of the law.[3] He saved the structure of the Supreme Court but doomed America to increasing regulation of business. In his dissent, Justice Sutherland wrote that "the meaning of the Constitution does not change with the ebb and flow of economic events." Yet after *West Coast Hotel*, the Constitution was held to allow government regulation of business for economic reasons.

The switch was immediate and absolute. In 1938, FDR signed the Agricultural Adjustment Act regulating the amount of wheat that farmers could plant, with the hope of stabilizing the price of that commodity. The Act was justified under the Interstate Commerce Clause of the Constitution. In 1941, an Ohio farmer named Roscoe Filburn planted more than his state-directed allotment of wheat. The excess was not sold, however, but used for private consumption on Filburn's farm, so no commerce had taken place. Filburn was prosecuted in the name of the Secretary of Agriculture, Claude Wickard.

In *Wickard v. Filburn* (1942), the Supreme Court, now with eight Roosevelt appointees, found that despite no actual commerce having taken place, Filburn's breach of his allotment did affect interstate commerce because it meant that he would buy less feed from the national market, and that if others did what Filburn did, interstate commerce would be affected that way. The Commerce Clause thereby became the justification for federal regulation of just about every aspect of business.

Thanks to *Wickard*, if a volunteer at a winery picks up a phone, he is subject to federal employment regulations, because the phone call might be about an aspect of interstate commerce. *Wickard* has also been used to justify the federal prosecution of people who grow medical marijuana for their own use, regardless of state laws that allow the practice.[4] It was also central to the arguments for the constitutionality of the Affordable Care Act (Obamacare). All for the collective good.

Of course, for regulation of the economy you need bureaucrats. The New Deal saw a plethora of new agencies modeled after those of the Progressive Era. Known as the "alphabet soup" or "alphabet agencies," some were short-lived (including the Civil Works Administration, which provided short-term make-work jobs for manual workers) and others are still with us today (such as the Securities and Exchange Commission). Many were created by executive order; the National Industrial Recovery Act (NIRA) of 1933 gave the president broad powers to do so, allocating the then enormous sum of $3.3

billion to create the National Recovery Administration (NRA) and the Public Works Administration.

The NRA in particular was highly controversial. It spewed out price controls and regulations by the bucketload, creating "codes of fair competition" and giving workers a say in the running of businesses (does that sound familiar?). It proved very popular with large segments of Americans, and businesses that did not display the NRA's "Blue Eagle" symbol could be the subject of boycotts.

Yet, as always with price controls and excessive regulation, the proof of the economic pudding was in the eating. Black markets grew up in many industries. Entrepreneurs who dared to offer goods for less than the price controls allowed were arrested. Night work was a particular target. As John T. Flynn explains, "Flying squadrons of these private coat-and-suit police went through the district at night, battering down doors with axes looking for men who were committing the crime of sewing together a pair of pants at night." Critics accused the enforcement officials of acting like stormtroopers.[5]

In a last gasp for the Lochner Era and a reasonable interpretation of the Commerce Clause, the Supreme Court shut down the NRA as unconstitutional in 1935, also holding that the NIRA was an unconstitutional delegation of Congress's legislative power to the president.

Bureaucracy, however, will not be denied. The same year that the Court upbraided Congress for delegating power to the president, it said that it was fine to delegate legislative power to what we now call independent agencies. In this case it was the Federal Trade Commission. In a case titled *Humphrey's Executor v. United States*, the Court decided that the president did not have the power to remove a member of the Commission—Commissioner Humphrey, who was unenthusiastic about the New Deal—on account of policy differences.[6]

While at the time it looked like the Court was standing up to a dictatorial president, the case has taken on a much different meaning over the years. The ruling in *Humphrey's Executor* enabled Congress to set up a whole bunch of agencies to issue regulations knowing that at best the president would have only indirect control over them through the appointment of commissioners. In recent years, Congress has dispensed with the multi-member commission model entirely and created agencies with a single director unremovable by the president.

As the bureaucracy grew, expropriations gathered speed. A series of Revenue Acts and other measures during the New Deal introduced all sorts of new taxes, including the "Wealth Tax" of 1935, which took 75 percent of high incomes. It wasn't all soak the rich; however, social security taxes were introduced, affecting all earners. Not all the taxes proved sustainable. A tax on undistributed profits was repealed in the late thirties. But the Second World War, with its need for substantial revenue, cemented many New Deal taxes in place.

There was also actual expropriation of property, not just income. In 1933, Executive Order 6012 in made it illegal for Americans to own or trade above $100 worth of gold (with exceptions for jewelry, coin collections, and dentistry). The Gold Reserve Act of 1934 forced Americans to hand over their gold for compensation at about twenty dollars an ounce. After the expropriation, FDR raised the price of gold to thirty-five dollars an ounce by proclamation, effectively devaluing the U.S. dollar but substantially increasing federal reserves.

A lot more could be said about the New Deal. I would recommend reading *The Forgotten Man* by Amity Shlaes, a painstaking history of what the poet Auden called a "low, dishonest decade." Suffice it say that there were elements of both Stalin and Mussolini in FDR's approach.[7]

As for socialism, the New Deal didn't go in for outright nationalization of industries, but Roosevelt's imposition of price controls and regulation by law and decree seem to be good examples of what people today mean when they talk about socialism. The debate over FDR's legacy has been going on since the early days of the New Deal, but if America ever had a socialist president, he was it.

By the end of the New Deal, America effectively had two constitutions in place. There was the original that can be carried around in a pocket and enumerated the limited powers of the federal government, and there was a much longer one made up of what have been called "super-statutes" that had been passed during the Progressive Era (such as the Sherman Act, regulating antitrust) and the New Deal (such as the Wagner Act, giving privileges to unions). The courts would come to treat these super-statutes as if they had constitutional significance. To this day, these grants of legislative and discretionary power to the executive and the federal bureaucracy are almost impossible to repeal. This second constitution is the rock on which any socialist administration would build its power.

CHAPTER 4

What Do the Polls Tell Us?

S o what do we know about Americans' attitudes toward socialism today? The answer is not much, surprisingly. We do know
that it is becoming more popular than capitalism, both from
polls, and from the fact that the number of people who have joined
socialist organizations or who read socialist publications has gone
up. Beyond that, however, emerges a picture of an America deeply
confused about what socialism really is.

Let's take political activism first. At the end of the Cold War, the
Democratic Socialists of America had just six thousand members.
According to *Reason* magazine's Robby Soave, the Democratic Socialists' magazine had just 6,700 subscribers as recently as 2016.[1] But
boosted by the presidential campaign of Democratic Socialist Party
member Bernie Sanders, that number jumped to 28,000 in 2017, and
then—presumably thanks to the emergence of superstar member
AOC—to 46,000 in 2018.

Moreover, while progressives built huge media empires such as
DailyKos and *Vox* in the 2000s, now the overtly socialist *Jacobin*
magazine, founded in 2010 and named after the murderous French

revolutionaries, appears to be the place for the fresh-faced young radical to go. It has a print circulation of forty thousand and over a million online page views per month. (Its editor, Bhaskar Sunkara, has helpfully provided a distillation of his views in book form. *The Socialist Manifesto* is a conscious nod to *The Communist Manifesto* of Marx and Engels, but is, it has to be said, not without humor. I'll refer to it a lot.)

But these numbers are small, in the great scheme of things. To understand why socialism is the big thing these days, we need to look at polling numbers.

When it comes to the popularity of socialism among Democrats, a 2019 survey by the Cato Institute found a strong swing towards socialism and away from capitalism after the election of President Trump.[2] In 2016, slightly more Democrats were favorable to capitalism than to socialism—58 percent to 56 percent. By 2019, that had swung sharply: 64 percent were favorable to socialism and only 46 percent to capitalism. Fifty percent of Democrats admitted that their view of the president had made them less sympathetic to capitalism.

Favorable attitudes toward socialism can also be seen among the identity groups that affiliate most closely with Democrats—African Americans, young people, and lower-income Americans. Those groups saw favorability towards socialism ratings of 62 percent, 49 percent, and 50 percent respectively. Hispanics, however, were much more favorable to capitalism than to socialism—52 to 36 percent.

The swing the Cato Institute identified is also visible in the Gallup Poll figures.[3] In 2012, 2014, and 2016 both capitalism and socialism were viewed favorably by around 55 percent of Democrats, give or take a few points. In 2018 a ten-point gap opened up, with 57 percent favorable to socialism and 47 percent to capitalism.

What these figures suggest is that socialism hasn't so much gained ground as capitalism has lost it. It is particularly interesting to note that, according to Gallup, 68 percent of young people eighteen to twenty-nine held a favorable view of capitalism in 2010, two years after the financial crisis, but by 2018 that number had plummeted to 45 percent. Young people's favorability towards socialism held steady at 51 percent. Older Americans, including those aged thirty to forty-nine, continue to favor capitalism by about twenty points, while favorability towards socialism among Americans fifty or older languishes at 30 percent or less. Another poll, by news organization Axios, found that across young people aged eighteen to twenty-four, socialism was more popular than capitalism by 61 percent to 58 percent—the only age segment in which that was true.[4]

Since the preference for socialism over capitalism is driven by young people and Democrats, we should look more closely at what those groups think. Again, Gallup has some useful recent data.[5] Non-Hispanic white Democrats, particularly those with a college degree only, have become much more liberal over the past two decades.

This means that, even as Democrats have become less white as a party, and non-whites are less likely to identify as politically liberal than whites, "nonwhites' influence on Democrats' ideology is more than offset by the expanding proportion of college-educated Democrats—the latter being among the most liberal of all Democratic subgroups."

Moreover, when it comes to policies, Democrats tend to agree on economic policies and disagree on social policies. It is those economic policies that can fairly be described as socialist in one way or another: policies aimed at reducing income inequality, strengthening labor unions, and controlling emissions to combat global warming, for example. Only when it comes to government-run healthcare is there disagreement between liberal and moderate-conservative Democrats over a policy that is essentially socialist.

Harvard Kennedy School's Institute of Politics (IoP) has further useful data about the popularity of socialist policies among young Americans eighteen to twenty-nine years old. As the subheader for the release of their Fall 2018 Youth Poll exclaims, "Majorities Support Democratic Socialist Policies around Health Care, Education, and Jobs."[6]

The poll found strong support for a variety of policies usually advanced by candidates who identify themselves as democratic socialists, especially among the young people who are likely voters:

- 67 percent supported "Single Payer Health Care (also referred to as Medicare for all) where the federal government would cover all the health care expenses of individuals" (Notably, this contrasts with Gallup's finding about Democratic voters in general)
- 53 percent supported "[r]equiring U.S. corporations with more than $1 billion in revenue to allow their workers to elect 40 percent of the membership of their board of directors"
- 62 percent favored "[e]liminating tuition and fees at public four-year colleges and universities for students from families that make up to $125,000 per year and making community college tuition free for all income levels"
- 47 percent were in support of "[b]uilding a militant and powerful labor movement in the United States rooted in the multiracial working class"
- 63 percent were even in favor of a "federal jobs guarantee that would provide funding so that every American would be guaranteed a job paying at least $15 an hour and offering paid family/sick leave and health benefits"

With the exception of the question of labor unions, all of these policies go way beyond anything proposed by a mainstream liberal candidate, at least in recent memory. They are radical policies, revolutionary even, which would have huge implications for the way American society operates.

But perhaps the most illuminating result was when the IoP asked about support for capitalism, socialism, and democratic socialism. The young respondents favored these positions by 43 percent, 31 percent, and 39 percent respectively.

The IoP gave some respondents definitions of the different economic systems before asking the favorability question. The definitions were:

Capitalism: "An economic system characterized by private or corporate ownership of capital goods, by investments that are determined by private decision, and by prices, production, and the distribution of goods that are determined mainly by competition in a free market."

Socialism: "Any of various economic and political theories advocating collective or governmental ownership and administration of the means of production and distribution of goods."

Democratic Socialism: "A political philosophy that advocates achieving socialist goals within a democratic system."

In comparison with the sample who were just asked the question straight, support for capitalism surged and support for socialism plummeted when these definitions were given. Support for democratic socialism remained about the same. When informed, 54 percent of young people supported capitalism, 24 percent socialism, and 37 percent democratic socialism.

Combined with the Gallup results, the IoP results point us towards a coherent picture of what young, white, college-educated Americans mean when they talk about socialism.

The most important point is that our young socialists are more interested in the outcomes promised by socialism than in the means of achieving it. State ownership and direction of the "commanding heights of the economy"—as Lenin called them—are not at the top of their wish list. What they want is essentially a welfare state, but a more expansive version of the welfare state than anywhere in the world. Free college and worker participation on boards are hallmarks of European social democracies, but single-payer health systems like Canada's are outliers (most European countries have a system of private insurers and hospitals combined with government subsidies).[7] A "jobs guarantee" goes further still. In recent years such guarantees have been adopted only in developing countries like India and South Africa. Their long-term effects are as yet-unproven but in India, for example, they have centered on low-skill manual labor such as for government works projects, much like the short-lived New Deal program.[8]

As for labor unions, today mass membership is confined mostly to the Nordic social democracies (Sweden, Denmark, and Finland all had over 75 percent of employees as union members in 2000). Germany and the United Kingdom have about a quarter of their workforces enrolled in labor unions, while France, at 9 percent, is even lower than America, at 13 percent. (All figures are as of the year 2000.[9]) There is no requirement that a "militant and powerful" labor movement should represent a majority of employees, of course, but in those countries where labor unions are an integral part of employment and company management, militancy is somewhat unusual. (We discuss unions in greater detail below.)

For young supporters of socialism, socialism is about fairness and equality rather than revolution and public ownership. In fact, this modern redefinition of socialism is reflected in the understanding of the term by the nation as a whole. A Gallup poll from October

2018 asked people what they thought was meant by socialism, helpfully asking the very same question as they had done in 1949.

Just after World War II, 34 percent of Americans thought socialism meant "Government ownership or control, government ownership of utilities, everything controlled by the government, state control of business." Only one in eight Americans at that time thought that socialism was about "Equality—equal standing for everybody, all equal in rights, equal in distribution."

Today, those numbers have flipped. In 2018 just under a quarter favored the "equality" definition, and only 17 percent thought socialism meant government control. Ten percent took the welfare state approach: "Benefits and services—social services free, medicine for all" (a position that barely registered back in 1949, at 2 percent). The percentage holding that socialism is communism hasn't changed, at 6 percent. Whether that's positively or negatively meant wasn't part of the survey.

Democrats, as we might expect given what we've learned so far, are more likely to take the equality-welfare position—just under 40 percent of Democrats espouse either of those definitions, as opposed to 19 percent who think that socialism is about government. Yet even among Republicans, those definitions are popular: 29 percent of GOP supporters or leaners think socialism is about government control or is simply communism, but 30 percent adhere to the equality or welfare state definition.

Gallup's Dr. Frank Norwood sums it up: "These results make it clear that socialism is a broad concept that can be—and is—understood in a variety of ways by Americans. Republicans, who are overwhelmingly negative about socialism, tend to skew toward seeing socialism as government control of the economy and in derogatory terms, while Democrats, a majority of whom are positive about socialism, are more likely to view it as government provision of services."[10]

Many of our democratic socialists seem genuinely to believe that the socialism they espouse is different from the socialism of the old Communist bloc. As we'll see, this is an example of what a Marxist might call "false consciousness." All those nations of the old Communist bloc started out with the same promises of equality, democracy, and a better life for all. What doomed them all was the internal contradictions of socialist economics. The results were tragic.

Moreover, despite all of the talk about modern socialism being something different, we shouldn't lose sight of the fact that a quarter of young people, making up about two-thirds of those who espouse "democratic socialism," still support the idea of government control of the economy. Given that we are talking about college-educated young people as being most favorable to socialism, we should look at where they're getting their ideas.

CHAPTER 5

Socialism on Campus

One place you have to look if you want to understand socialism in America is the American college campus. If you were lucky enough to go to college twenty years ago or more, you probably remember that experience fondly. You likely learned about your major in depth without experiencing much of an ideological agenda on the part of the faculty.

While the professoriate has always had a leftward tilt (at least since we started measuring ideology in the sixties), the split was about 40 percent left or liberal, 30 percent moderate, and 30 percent conservative until around the year 2000.[1]

Since 2001, however, the proportion of leftist professors has significantly and steadily increased, and the number of conservatives similarly decreased, leading to a 60–30–10 split in the most recent years. Moreover, the number of professors identifying as "far left," which had always held steady at about 5 percent (we all remember those shoeless, open-shirted types who insisted on your calling them by their first name and seemed disturbingly interested in their female students) has more than doubled, to just under 12 percent today. That means that the far left has more of a voice in American teaching than all stripes of conservatives.

As we ponder these numbers, we should remember that a lot of fields of study are, thankfully, not particularly vulnerable to political influence. Engineering, for example, can only allow so much discussion of gender influence on fluid dynamics. That means, though, that the politically inclined professors are much more concentrated in certain subjects. Economic historian Phil Magness found that over 80 percent of English faculty identify as on the left. He also discovered that "[s]ubjects such as history, political science, sociology, and fine arts typically approach or exceed 70 percent. In short, the humanities and social sciences have become ideological monoliths."

This has had a serious effect on scholarship in those areas, of course. It has now become almost a parlor game to get hoax articles accepted for publication in what used to be respected scholarly journals. One trio of researchers literally made a study of this problem, writing hoax papers specifically to get them published. They summarized their methods: "The goal was always to use what the existing literature offered to get some little bit of lunacy or depravity to be acceptable at the highest levels of intellectual respectability within the field. Therefore, each paper began with something absurd or deeply unethical (or both) that we wanted to forward or conclude. We then made the existing peer-reviewed literature do our bidding in the attempt to get published in the academic canon."[2]

In seven cases they succeeded, in one case gaining "special recognition" (for a paper entitled "Human Reactions to Rape Culture and Queer Performativity in Urban Dog Parks in Portland, Oregon"). Several other papers were under serious consideration when the project's purpose was revealed. The authors of the fake research were often invited to review other papers.

While the researchers are adamant that the journal review process is mostly sound, they did find clear signs of political influence: "Look at the reviewer comments and what they are steering academics who need to be published to succeed in their careers towards. See how frequently they required us not to be less politically biased and shoddy in our work but more so."

That bias is all in one direction—towards socialist and associated conclusions.

The kind of socialism college professors favor is also important. It is generally classic Marxism. There is no better indication of this than the prescribed reading of Marx himself, in particular of his *Communist Manifesto*.

Thanks to a new open-source project called Open Syllabus, Phil Magness was able to look at the most assigned texts in American college courses. Excluding textbooks and style manuals, far and away the most prescribed text in 2016 was *The Communist Manifesto*— outstripping Plato, Aristotle, Hobbes, and John Stuart Mill.[3] Plato has made a comeback in the most recent figures, but not by much (*The Republic* was assigned 7088 times to 7057 for *The Communist Manifesto*.[4])

Moreover, students aren't told to read Marx in just economics or political science classes, where the assignment is certainly justifiable, but in many other disciplines. Out of all 7057 assignments, 1830 were in history, 747 in English literature, 600 in philosophy, and only 179 in economics. In 2017 alone, out of 527 syllabi, 87 assignments were in history courses and 66 in English literature. It need hardly be said that *The Communist Manifesto* is not the most sparkling work of English literature, having the unfortunate handicap of being written in German.

Marx is being thrust down the throats of our college students. It is only to be expected that they will vomit back socialism. While the politics of college students as a whole reflect those of the country, being evenly split between left-liberals, moderates, and conservatives, students in those fields where Marx is assigned most often are much more likely to think favorably of socialism. Magness points to a College Pulse survey of ten thousand undergraduates that found eight in ten philosophy majors had a favorable view of socialism (four in ten *very* favorable), alongside six in ten English majors. For economics, the figure is just 26 percent, with 61 percent viewing it unfavorably.[5]

Magness, an economist, is scathing on the process by which this happens. He points to Georgetown University philosopher Jason Brennan's work that suggests that philosophers tend to talk about socialist ideals, then use those ideals to point out the failings of the largely capitalist society around them—without considering the failings of socialist societies: "An economist who studies prices, scarcity, and trade-offs has a direct professional awareness of economic policy making, and with it the untenable nature of socialist economic planning.... But what training does a literature professor have that permits him or her to competently opine on economic regulation, on tax policy, on public finance and budgeting, or on centrally planned resource allocation by the state? How about the creative-writing professor? Or the fine arts professor? The Spanish or German professor?"[6]

The result is that humanities students are getting a seriously defective introduction to economic and political realities, based on easily falsifiable assertions that their professors do not bother to critique. Because of the dynamics discussed above, they are not challenged on this by their peers. The result is an echo chamber.

When professors who actually do know what they are talking about put up a fuss, it can have no effect. Duke University historian Nancy MacLean was feted by her profession for writing a tendentious and biased assessment of the work of Nobel prize–winning economist James Buchanan, asserting that his "public choice" school of economics was essentially just a front for racism. Her book *Democracy in Chains* has won a ton of awards.

Duke economist Michael Munger actually knows something about public choice economics and knew Buchanan personally. In his lengthy and devastating review of MacLean's book, Munger points out that no fewer than three prominent members of Duke's political science faculty knew and worked with Buchanan, and suggests, "In short, I would expect that a sophomore undergraduate who is writing a paper on Buchanan, even a one-off paper for a classroom assignment, would recognize the value in consulting Brennan, at a minimum, and probably also Vanberg.... But neither Brennan nor Vanberg were ever consulted, nor even contacted, by MacLean. Nor, if it matters, was I." [7]

MacLean accused her critics of a "coordinated campaign" that amounted to "rhetorical bullying." [8] She attacked their *bona fides* and hand-waved away their scholarship as a politically motivated attack. Following Munger's review, she told her followers on social media, "This will sound nutty, I know, but it's actually happening: the Koch operatives and the riders of their academic 'gravy train,' as James Buchanan called it, are working very hard to kill Democracy in Chains—and to destroy my reputation (as they have done to climate change scientists and others bearing inconvenient truth)." [9] To date, she has not addressed Munger's substantive criticism.

The spoon-feeding of socialism to students and the arrogance towards colleagues go hand in hand with disdain for other points of view. The Foundation for Individual Rights in Education (FIRE) has catalogued case after case of students (and even professors) being harassed for expressing unorthodox (that is, conservative) points of view. As you might expect from the figures presented above, the crisis over free speech on college campuses is at its worst in small liberal arts colleges, where humanities faculty make up the bulk of the staff.

Conversely, students who do subscribe to the orthodoxy are protected from having their views challenged. Colleges have put a variety of protections in place for students who want to shut down debate—or avoid confronting difficult ideas in the first place (that's why this book has a trigger warning). FIRE president George Lukianoff and social scientist Jonathan Haidt call this "the coddling of the American mind."[10] Plato's mentor Socrates was put to death by the Athenians for his alarming habit of asking difficult questions. His accusers' spiritual heirs make up the governing class of today's universities—that's Socratic irony for you.

In short, America's colleges and universities have turned their humanities programs into factories for churning out young socialists. Armed with an insufferable sense of their own superiority and a disdain for anyone who would challenge their ideology, they are taking this worldview into their working and family lives.

As we've seen, it is this demographic segment that is the vanguard of resurgent socialism. Yet it is entirely plausible that their arguments and preferred policies will be presented as a choice to Americans in a presidential election (if not in 2020, then soon). To understand why that is even possible, we need to look at how socialism appeals to the values that underlie American politics.

CHAPTER 6

Cultural Cognition and American Values

T his book is not a detailed critique of socialism past and present. If you are looking for an explanation of why socialism doesn't work as an economic system, you will not find that here. For that, I recommend the recent Regnery book *Socialism Sucks* by Robert Lawson and Benjamin Powell. It's a tale of two economists drinking their way through the unfree world, and it's a great look at how socialism affects the countries that have tried it.

My concern is, *why is socialism so alluring to modern Americans?* As we've seen, it is, more now than at any point in history. But *why?*

To understand this phenomenon, I believe we need to delve into a field of study called Cultural Cognition. Deriving in large part from the academic work of Mary Douglas and the late Aaron Wildavsky, a friend of my mentor Fred Smith, research into Cultural Cognition suggests that there is a relationship between the values we hold and how we perceive risk. How we perceive gun crime, for example, depends on whether a proposed solution to gun crime threatens our values. As different political ideologies offer packages of solutions to risks, our values make those ideologies more or less attractive to us.

According to Wildavsky, America is made up of four main value groups:

- *Hierarchists.* A hierarchist (from the Greek-derived word hierarchy, rule by priests) views order and stability as of primary importance. Social relationships are defined by everything being where it should be (such as in church or the military). Many American conservatives are hierarchists. As hierarchist is an awkward and unfamiliar term, and as most hierarchist American conservatives value tradition, from now on I'll refer to hierarchists as traditionalists.
- *Egalitarians.* The egalitarian's primary value is fairness. Community is as important to the egalitarian as it is to the hierarchist, but equality within the community is vital, which means that differing outcomes as a result of public policy are anathema. Most American progressives are egalitarians.
- *Individualists.* For the individualist, the primary value is liberty. Social relationships are viewed as networks of individuals connected to one another. Many American conservatives are individualists.
- *Fatalists.* Fatalists believe their life is determined by chance and luck, so insofar as they have a value, it is good luck. Their social relationships are best described as tenuous. Fatalists are probably more likely to play the lottery than to be involved in politics; they tend not to vote. For this reason, I won't be discussing fatalism much in this book. Occasionally a political leader can co-opt groups of fatalists to his side through demagoguery. Those demagogues can be from left or right, but

they have been much more prevalent outside the United States (despite what some people might tell you).[1]

Naturally, these groups' ideas of the best political system will differ. The individualist, for instance, likes a society with a high degree of individual autonomy and a low degree of collective action. By contrast, the traditionalist would prefer a society with a great deal of collective action and a low degree of personal autonomy.

Egalitarians would like to have it both ways, with individual autonomy and collective action both important, the collective action being determined by consensus in order to square the circle.

One way of thinking about these values is that together they make up the American Dream: a fair society free from privilege, where individuals can flourish according to their own merit, within a community they are happy to see their children grow up in. The fact that we have differing emphases within this dream is where political disagreements arise. At first blush, it may seem that these value groups map neatly onto American politics—Democrats, Republicans, and libertarians, who have been in political alliance with the Republicans for many decades. But as in most of life, it's not as simple as that. Union households, for instance, put a lot of store by tradition and order.

This is why most successful political movements work by appealing to more than one value group. Welfare reform in the Clinton era came about because it appealed to all three value groups:

- Individualists felt that excessive welfare was a waste of taxpayers' money
- Traditionalists were worried that welfare had perverse consequences that were leading to the demise of the family

- Egalitarians eventually came to realize that excessive welfare without a work requirement was actually hurting the poor

This meant that welfare reform was a no-brainer. It was a win-win-win.

It could be touted as a success by both the liberal President Clinton and the conservative Congress led by Newt Gingrich.

More recent reforms have not achieved the same buy-in by value groups. Obamacare, for instance, was rammed through Congress on the principle that it would lead to fairer outcomes for the previously uninsured, but it upended the traditional insurance system—resulting in much higher healthcare costs—and significantly reduced the amount of individual choice (Don't want to buy a plan that covers contraception because you're a Catholic nun? Tough luck!).

On the other hand, financial regulation such as Dodd–Frank has proved difficult to dislodge because the system that led to the financial crisis was viewed as flawed by every group. Egalitarians felt that the system had exploited people who lost their homes. Traditionalists regarded the system as disruptive, creating a *nouveau riche* class that disregarded traditional moral principles like thrift. Individualists hated the way the banks seemed greedy for bailouts. So, despite the fact that not all the groups agreed with the nature of the reforms, there was an agreement that reform was needed.

Don't forget that most voters are not particularly politically sophisticated. They have no interest in economic calculus or cost-benefit analysis. Many, as Fred Smith often pointed out, don't even know the identity of their senator, never mind their congressman—let alone their representatives' views on particular political issues.

That is why appealing to values is so important politically. The politicians must show they care about what their constituents care about. In response to any suggestion that the voter was just stupid, Fred would respond: *They're not stupid because they're stupid, they're stupid because they're smart, and if you try to make them smart, you're being stupid.*

He was referring to a phenomenon that social scientists call "rational ignorance": because voters don't have time to become experts on everything, attempts by aspiring politicos to make voters experts generally fall flat. You may remember Al Gore's Oscar-winning film *An Inconvenient Truth*, which attempted to make voters "smart" about global warming. Fifteen years later, a Swedish schoolgirl had much more impact because she appealed to values, not to climate science.[2]

The message to egalitarians is that global warming will harm the poor disproportionately. To traditionalists the message is that global warming will harm God's creation and wreck the heritage we need to preserve for our children. Individualists have been a trickier challenge, but activists have argued, increasingly successfully, that the market can solve the problem if it is incentivized by measures such as carbon taxes, rather than emissions caps. Even self-styled libertarian think tanks now accept that argument (although, thankfully, most individual, err, individualists do not). Donors have poured huge resources into values-based messaging on this issue, resulting in such initiatives as the appropriately named Yale Project on Cultural Cognition.

Moreover, as the economist Arnold Kling has pointed out, the three groups speak different languages when it comes to politics.[3] This means that messaging can signal to the value groups that it is something they should care about by using the language of the groups.

The egalitarian speaks in terms of oppressors and the oppressed. As Kling points out, a member of an oppressed group can be given a free pass for what might seem to be oppression, while some who complain about oppression will be ignored because they are members of an oppressor group (Kling gives the example of conservative students denied free speech on campus).

Traditionalists have a different viewpoint. They view the struggle as between civilization and barbarism. Those who defend tradition are seen as upholding civilization, even when their personal conduct might be viewed as uncivilized.

As for the individualists, they view the conflict as between freedom and coercion. So the libertarian might side with the egalitarian over the traditionalist on the question of police powers (the libertarian viewing "stop and search" as coercive, the egalitarian viewing it as racist, but the traditionalist seeing it as upholding the rule of law), but with the traditionalist on the question of campus speech.

Kling's point, by the way, is not about messaging at all, but rather how looking at an issue from one viewpoint is lazy and contributes to political problems. He would prefer it if we all slowed down and looked at issues from the other points of view from our own. That's good advice. But my point is that the axes of political language are important for seeing just how an ideology like socialism and the policies it entails can appeal to so many different people.

Socialist solutions can be advanced as part of an agenda that is not nominally socialist. Thus socialism, in its manifold varieties, can appeal to all American value groups.

It appeals to the egalitarian for obvious reasons. It promises equality of outcomes and an end to oppression by exploitative forces. It claims to be democratic, so that decisions will be reached by consensus. Throughout socialism's sordid history, egalitarians have been the most prone to the socialist temptation. Even the great George Orwell, who knew how socialism could turn so easily into totalitarianism, continued to regard himself as a democratic socialist because he was an egalitarian.

Yet time and again, egalitarians have been cheated by socialism. The society they end up with is just as unequal and divided as the one it replaced—"Meet the new boss, same as the old boss," as The Who put it. The promise of democratic consensus proves illusory. Whether it's the Paris Commune or Stalin's purges, the system always fails to ensure equality.

Socialism also speaks the language of liberty. Its advocates claim to be the real defenders of freedom. They argue that a man can only be free when socialism ends oppression—"Workers of the world unite! You have nothing to lose but your chains!" This vision has been extremely seductive. Socialist terrorists around the world have called themselves "freedom fighters."

Some self-styled libertarians have begun to argue that agency— the ability to pursue one's goals without constraints such as lack of money—is the only true freedom. So, they argue, government must provide a Universal Basic Income (UBI) to enable agency, which requires good old socialist redistribution of wealth.[4]

But freedom, like equality, is elusive in actual socialist systems. The agency of having a bit more money under socialism to spend when unemployed turns out not to be worth much—in a very literal sense. Prices rise and supply contracts. Opportunity disappears, innovation and entrepreneurialism fizzle, and the only hope for advancement is becoming a bureaucrat.

Then there is tradition; perhaps nowhere in recent years has the rise of socialist thought been as surprising as among some self-styled conservatives. They have been seduced into thinking that socialist policies can support their values. Free trade, of which Ronald Reagan was a champion because of the prosperity he realized it brought, has been blamed for all manner of woes befalling the American heartland. Large companies are attacked for failing to stand up for traditional values. If the market fails to provide jobs, it is criticized for not valuing the importance of work to the family and community.

All these complaints may have a degree of merit about them. Yet the solutions advanced are socialist ones: autarkic commerce, ferocious antitrust enforcement, and redistribution of wealth. Their proponents may deny that the ideas are socialist—deny it until they are blue in the face in some cases—but the fact remains that the policies are those that traditional socialists would recognize and claim as their own.

British Conservatives of a certain age should recognize this problem. From 1948 to 1979, the British Conservative party bought into the democratic socialist nationalized economy that was created after the Second World War. It was felt that dismantling nationalized industries would be too disruptive of communities. When Margaret Thatcher embarked on her program of privatization, that did prove to be the case. Communities were indeed disrupted as traditional sources of male employment disappeared. My own hometown saw massive unemployment as the shipbuilding and coal mining industries shut down—at one point only half of all men of working age had a job. Yet over the years, the community proved resilient, as free enterprise worked its magic. While still higher than the national unemployment rate of 4.1 percent, my hometown's male unemployment rate is now 7 percent.

This book, however, is about America. In the remainder of this book I will examine how socialism and socialist policies appeal to each of the three main values groups I have outlined. My treatment of the appeal of socialism to each value group will start with a summary of the socialist position in relation to that group's values, followed by a look at whether the socialist claims hold up (hint—they don't) and then proceed to suggestions for alternative policies that better accord with these great American values.

Finally, I will attempt to tie this all together and demonstrate that socialism is a temptation we cannot afford to indulge. In particular, I will show how the current conservative strife over policy risks everything conservatives hold dear.

As former Redskins coach George Allen liked to say, "The future is now."[5] Conservatives cannot afford to descend to infighting or, worse, adopting their enemies' policies at a time when the threat is the greatest it has been for a generation.

If the socialist temptation is not resisted, the very future of America is in jeopardy. The stakes could not be higher.

PART TWO

Can Socialism Deliver a Fair Society?

CHAPTER 7

The Socialist Position

E quality is central to the socialist argument. A modern-day socialist may put the argument something like this.

A socialist believes in equality. Equality takes many forms.

Equality between the classes: the roots of the socialist movement are in the class struggle. Capitalists took over a pre-existing form of inequality between aristocrats and feudal peasants and reworked it to their own advantage, to the detriment of the peasantry. The holders of capital and property became the new ruling class, exploiting the labor of the working class and expropriating what property they had. Socialists led the way in creating the labor movement to reduce exploitation and win important protections for workers.

The American idea of the "middle class" is a result of those hard-won protections. Unions brought workers together to balance the power of business owners. Their collective bargaining ensured good wages, stable employment, and generous pension arrangements. Workers paid fair union dues to ensure that everyone had a stake in the system. The American dream of the 1950s was the result of this balance of power brought about by the labor movement. The unlucky few without unions were protected by New Deal laws such as the Fair Labor Standards Act.

The Reagan era began a process of steady dismantling of those pro-tections. Where wages were rising, they have stagnated. The vast explo-sion of wealth over the past few decades has been captured by the own-ers of capital, and workers have seen none of it. In the name of "eco-nomic growth," hard-won protections have been stripped away. Unions have been demonized. Successive tax cuts have delivered breadcrumbs for the workers and billions for the rich.

To remedy this situation, socialists turn to democracy. Economic institutions that affect the lives of workers and consumers should be controlled by those workers and consumers, within a framework of regulation designed to protect those outside the institution from harm-ful effects. This is in line with the earliest socialist thought: Marx and Engels talked of workers' control of factories.

Most modern socialists reject the idea of state ownership of busi-nesses except in a few crucial industries such as energy. Instead, they believe in decentralization so that decisions can be made by the work-ers and consumers closest to the effects of those decisions. So workers' cooperatives and similar forms of business should replace the private ownership model. This would also make the businesses less beholden to stockholder whims and more responsive to other needs, such as those of the environment.

Some socialists believe that "all property is theft," but they are few in number today. Outright collectivization of all property and the out-lawing of private property is not a position generally held by modern socialists. But large inheritance taxes should be used to minimize the unearned advantage of inherited capital.

Finally, in order to secure a safety net for those who are for what-ever reason unable to work in this new economic system, there should be generous welfare payments and a healthcare system that is free at the point of delivery. Increasing numbers of socialists believe that there should a universal basic income, guaranteed by government, to ensure that all citizens have an equal base income to help them through shorter or longer periods of unemployment.

Equality between the races: *Perhaps more problematic than class or income inequality is racial inequality. American slavery was uniquely evil and has led to persistent racial injustice that is also uniquely American. By every measure, African Americans are worse off than white Americans. Attempts to remediate these inequalities are hindered by the problem that the institutions involved were created and are to a large extent controlled by white people.*

Therefore racial inequalities cannot be reduced without tackling the problem of white privilege. Socialists realize that white people, even poor white people, have advantages over people of color that many of them cannot even recognize.

Socialism addresses this problem by stressing education and affirmative action. White people must be taught from childhood about their privilege and the costs it imposes on people of color. Affirmative action programs must be instituted to break down white privilege and ensure nondiscriminatory action by government officials and programs.

Equality between sexes and genders: *Just as there is a problem with white privilege, there is also a problem with society's privileging men, predominantly white men. This structure is known as the patriarchy.*

In particular, the patriarchy privileges men within the home. Women with children routinely bear most of the duties of child-rearing, however supportive their male partners. Motherhood makes them more dependent on their male partners for income, reinforcing the inequality.

Allowing women complete control over their reproductive choices is the first step in addressing this inequality—making easily available abortion a top priority for socialists. Guaranteeing childcare and paying women to stay at home are also important, closely followed by public education for older children.

Socialists also recognize a difference between sex and gender. So-called biological sex is not determinant of gender. Historically, people whose genders have not matched their sex have been persecuted and vilified. Equality for those of different genders also helps to undermine the patriarchy. That means that those who appear to be manifesting signs of different gender expression should be encouraged from a young age to do so. Moreover, thanks to the modern development of gender reassignment surgery, the surgery should be made available to those who need it, by public assistance if necessary.

The socialist temptation for the egalitarian is obvious. Insofar as you believe that these inequalities are something to worry about, the socialist position will promise attractive solutions. But stick around. We need to look at how socialism works in practice. As the British journalist Toby Young often puts it, "Socialism always begins with a universal vision for the brotherhood of man and ends with people having to eat their own pets."[1]

CHAPTER 8

The Gentleman in Washington, D.C., Knows Best

"In the case of nutrition and health, just as in the case of education, the gentleman in Whitehall really does know better what is good for people than the people know themselves," wrote British politician Peter Jay in *The Socialist Case* in 1937. Whitehall is the center of Britain's government, and Jay was arguing that the existence of inequality meant there was a role for central government planning.

In the same book Jay also said, "If there is an obligation on society to see that poor children should have medicine before a rich man has a cigar, there is an equally binding obligation to see that they should have milk.... In fact, where inequality is in question, we are as bound to depart from free consumers' choice as we are in education or health."

I use Jay as an example because in the 1930s he was what we might call a half-hearted socialist, who conceded a role for consumer choice and the private sector, tempered only by the concern for inequality displayed above. However, after the Second World War he became convinced by what he saw as the success of the wartime rationing program that central planning could work for everything.[1]

The post-war British socialist government, elected despite war hero Winston Churchill's warnings, proceeded to nationalize much of British industry, seizing the "commanding heights of the economy," a term borrowed from none other than Lenin. Yet the government's plans were stymied somewhat by Britain's essential bankruptcy following the war. Britain never became a Soviet-style planned economy with no significant private enterprise but got some of the way there.

Central planning is perhaps the original sin of socialism. Socialists claim that central planning has a scientific basis. The idea behind central planning is that "the gentleman in Whitehall" (or, in our case, Washington, D.C.) can accurately predict the amount of goods and services needed by the economy and plan for their delivery. How do they do that?

This was the first and most obvious problem faced by the new socialist systems of the 1920s, and it was instantly fingered as such by the Austrian economist Ludwig von Mises, who raised the question of "economic calculation" under socialism in an influential article, "Economic Calculation in the Socialist Commonwealth."[2]

The trouble is that economic calculation in a truly socialist system is basically impossible. Without private property, there are no markets that match supply and demand, and without markets there are no prices. Prices, which most people think are set arbitrarily by the seller, are actually the result of a huge amount of aggregated knowledge.[3] They contain information about scarcity, supply, demand, and consumer preferences.

Indeed it is prices that enable us to allocate resources efficiently and incentivize us to innovate. Without prices, I might as well spend time creating a gross of handcrafted onyx boomerangs as produce something people actually want (with apologies to the onyx boomerang artisans out there).

Socialism in its purest form gets rid of property, markets, and prices—and so ends up with a planning system based on the biases, judgment, and whims of the gentlemen in Washington.

This results in two outcomes that stand in stark contrast to the desire to reduce inequality.

First, the equality the socialist planning system delivers is one of equal immiseration (as we'll see in vivid detail when we discuss socialized health systems). In Venezuela, as Toby Young has pointed out, the failure of food distribution led to the widespread eating of pet rabbits.

Second, the gentlemen in Washington form a separate and unequal class, just as much a position of privilege as the aristocracy or the "Robber Barons." With the abolition of personal wealth, membership in this class is everything.

Perhaps this is why modern socialists will swear themselves blind that they aren't advocating for a planned economy. The Democratic Socialists of America say, "Democratic socialists have long rejected the belief that the whole economy should be centrally planned. While we believe that democratic planning can shape major social investments like mass transit, housing, and energy, market mechanisms are needed to determine the demand for many consumer goods."[4]

They are contradicting themselves here. Transportation, housing, and energy are just as much allocated by the price system as consumer goods. We already have "democratic" government interference with the system through such things as vehicle emissions standards, zoning, and fuel subsidies imposed by regulation. These distort price signals and lead to malinvestment and immiseration.

A hypothetical but perfectly plausible example: zoning could mean that I can't live close to work, so that I have to own a car, which is more expensive than I really need because of emissions standards.

Meanwhile I look over at my rich neighbor (a bureaucrat, perhaps?) who has an electric vehicle that is subsidized by my tax dollars. My household budget suffers as a result. That's the result of so-called "democratic" control of the system.

In a free market, I'd live close to work if that were my preference. If there were too many people wanting to live close to work, then developers would provide more housing to meet the demand. People would move in, helping the district thrive.[5] That's how New York became so densely populated. If there had been "democratic control" instead, there would probably be no skyscrapers, and a lot more of the city would look like the projects.

CHAPTER 9

Democratic Socialism in Action

Any review of genuine socialism would start with the Soviet Union—and quite possibly end with it, case closed. But Soviet-style socialism has never been attractive to the American voter. Abolition of private property is and will probably remain a step too far to be attractive to anyone except the stoned or the Middlebury student body. In that respect, modern American socialists are right that discussions of communism are irrelevant to their position.

Of course, that distinction often disappears when Venezuela, the victim of a Latin version of communism, is the subject of the discussion.

As we have already mentioned, no socialist system is erected on the understanding that it will lead to mass poverty, show trials, and the gulags. Yet they do tend to end up there, one way or another. Why does that happen? Because of the internal contradictions of socialism.

There are places where socialism works. They are small-scale and limited. The Israeli kibbutz is a great example. In the classic kibbutz, all decisions are taken collectively, property is owned communally, individuals rotate jobs, and equality is of paramount concern. Raising children in communal halls is seen as a way to promote women's equality, for instance.

However, part of the reason that socialism worked on kibbutzes (at least for a while—since the 1970s they have become more free market in approach) was their homogeneity. Kibbutzers bought in to the system for religious reasons. This was both a strength and a liability. Kibbutzes that suffered worker shortages employed Arab workers yet would not allow them to join the kibbutz.

Israel, however, is not a gigantic kibbutz, and never has been. Stalin approved the creation of Israel in the hope that it would become a socialist country but soon turned against it when he realized that hope was forlorn. Kibbutzes succeeded at least partly because they were distinct elements in a free-market system, competing not just with other kibbutzes but with traditional corporations and communities. Kibbutzes could not scale up to a national level.

The reasons for that are quite simple. Job rotation, for example, can work in a community where everyone knows and trusts everyone else, and where the tasks involved are simple enough that everyone can fulfill them. Rotating people in from outside raises problems of trust and competence. Some positions require expertise and dedication. The further you go from the local kibbutz model, the more intense these problems become.

Moreover, people are happy to live in kibbutzes because they have their voices heard. And should their voices not be heard, they have the option of leaving. They can go to another kibbutz, or to a community with more individual freedom.

At the national level, this doesn't work. Socialist countries cannot abide emigration. In *The Communist Manifesto* Marx and Engels suggested the "confiscation of the property of all emigrants and rebels." At least that would have allowed the dissident to emigrate, even if he could not take the proverbial suitcase. Countries that followed Marx had a tendency to treat potential emigrants more harshly. The Soviet Union sent dissidents to the gulags. East Germany constructed the Berlin Wall to prevent emigration; film footage of people being shot in their efforts to leave East Berlin is still hard to watch.

Europe's democratic socialist countries all suffered what was called the "brain drain," as gifted and highly educated individuals fled to escape punitive tax rates. Harold Wilson's Britain of the 1960s regarded this as a crisis, and it became a subject of major public debate. Today's social democracies are equally worried about what they call "base erosion," as people try to shift their tax liabilities to less confiscatory jurisdictions.

So if you cannot exit, where is your voice in the gigantic kibbutz of a socialist nation? In Eastern Bloc countries, the only voices heard were those of Communist Party officials—the gentlemen in Moscow.

In democratic socialist Britain things were slightly different. Because the major industries were nationalized and there was, at least until the 1970s, no democratic mandate for them to be privatized, the main voices in how those industries were run were political—the elected politicians who oversaw the industries and appointed their board members and also the labor union bosses who represented the workers in those industries. This was the Britain in which I grew up, and it is indelibly etched on my memory.

The main concern of the union bosses was more pay for their members. If the industry boards tried to cut back on pay, or even not offer enough in raises, the bosses would call their members out on strike. The unions would not just close down their own industry's facilities, though—other unions in other industries would strike "in sympathy," or the unions would picket other facilities in connected industries in what was called "secondary picketing." No union member worth his salt would ever dream of crossing a picket line, so the workers in those industries would essentially be forced to strike.

This was, of course, bad for the consumer. If you wanted to get to work during a railroad strike, tough luck. When the coal miners went on strike, the power station workers might come out in sympathy, and electricity would be shut off across the country (remember, these were nationalized industries). When I was small, the miners went on strike a lot, meaning I had to do my homework by candlelight in the evening. Where I grew up, many people's main source of heat was a coal fireplace. The hardship could be extraordinary by today's standards.

This made management of the industries by the politicians difficult. When times were hard, they would look to make cuts in service, such as the infamous "Beeching cuts" to railroad services that closed four of seven thousand rail stations across the country. When times were reasonably good, the unions would want their share of the pie, and demand more. Politicians would either concede to the unions, feeding into a vicious cycle of pay demands, or go to extraordinary lengths to avoid strikes by making other concessions to the unions, usually agreed over "beer and sandwiches" in 10 Downing Street, the Prime Minister's office.

And it wasn't just the strikes. The consumers were often the last thing on the industry board's minds. If you wanted to replace your coal fireplace with a natural gas heating system, for instance, you would have to go to a British Gas Corporation showroom, where you'd be shown an extremely limited choice of products (I remember traipsing round such showrooms with my parents).

Similarly, if you wanted a phone extension you would have to justify it to the Post Office (yes, the British General Post Office ran the phone network until the 1980s, with the postmaster-general, a cabinet minister, overseeing the whole thing.[1]) A friend of mine remembers his father being away on business trips a lot and his mother wanting a phone in her bedroom so that she could take the calls late at night. There were months of form-filling, applications, and bureaucracy before the request was granted. And you had a choice between the standard Post Office phone and the Space Age design "trimphone." That was it.

Once you had made your choice of heater or phone and gotten approval, there was a waiting list, of course. You could wait for months before something you had ordered from a nationalized industry was delivered. Waiting was also something that every customer of the British Rail system was used to.

There are simple economic reasons for all of this. When prices are not set by a market, supply and demand become disassociated. If there is too much demand and too little supply, then there is a rationing effect, which normally manifests in long waits for the service or product. Conversely, if there is too much supply and not enough demand, the product or service is essentially subsidized, and the cost of the subsidy will be borne by other customers or the taxpayer. Waiting lists are an example of the first case; Britain's over-reliance on coal as a source of fuel and the subsidies for fares on little-used railroad branch lines were examples of the latter.

Another burden on the consumer and the nation as a whole was a lack of innovation. Socialism doesn't mean that industries cannot be innovative—the Post Office partnered with AT&T and Bell Telephone to build Telstar, the world's first telecommunications satellite, in 1962—but by and large the lack of market economic incentives in socialism chills innovation. This is compounded by the "brain drain" effect discussed above. All this results in a general delay in the adoption of new ideas. The telephone wall jack, for example, was invented by private American firms in the 1960s, but the "new plan" for introducing them to the UK did not come about until the early 1980s, when the Thatcher government was preparing for privatization.

The pressures for reform by then were overwhelming. People had grown sick of the constant labor disputes disrupting their lives, to say nothing of the lack of choice and service. The quality of service on British Rail was exemplified by the proverbial "BR sandwich"—a thin slice of ham held between two curling pieces of stale bread. In 1970, Edward Heath was elected prime minister with a mandate to stand up to the unions. A couple of miners' and power workers' strikes and the forced imposition of a three-day work week led to his leaving office. The "democratic" part of democratic socialism was obviously secondary to the socialism.

Things reached a head in 1978–79's "Winter of Discontent," when the strikes were so widespread that piles of trash mounted up in urban streets as municipal garbage collectors stopped work for a month and even gravediggers went on strike for two weeks, leaving the dead unburied (the gravediggers got a 14 percent pay raise out of it). Even ambulance drivers and 999 operators (the British equivalent of 911) refused to work. Egalitarianism had resulted in equal misery for everyone except the public sector worker.

The public was so disgusted that they elected Margaret Thatcher to solve the problem. She broke the labor unions' stranglehold on the British economy.

That's what life was like in a relatively benign, partly democratic socialist state like the United Kingdom. In others, where the democratic element was far smaller, the results were much, much worse.

CHAPTER 10

The Socialist Death Toll

In the late 1920s, Iosif Dzhugashvili, known to the world as Stalin, faced a problem. A class of prosperous peasants, the *kulaks*, were agitating against the Soviet Revolution. To deal with these "class enemies," Stalin announced "the liquidation of kulaks as a class" and collectivized their farms. Some of the kulaks were simply to be shot, others sent to Siberia, and the rest relocated to work camps within the new collectives.

Those new collectives were burdened with an impressive array of rules, including production quotas. Even the new collective property was to be confiscated if certain benchmarks were not met. The first Five Year Plan ordered the farms to switch from their usual crops of grain to things such as sugar beets.

The results were horrific, particularly in the Ukrainian Soviet Socialist Republic in the early 1930s. The 1932 harvest was just over half the size of the previous year's. Rationing was imposed in cities, and the rations then swiftly cut. Western journalists such as Britain's Malcolm Muggeridge could see what was happening. He wrote in the *Manchester Guardian*, "The population is starving. 'Hunger' was the word I heard most. Peasants begged a lift on the train from one station to another sometimes their bodies swollen up—a disagreeable sight—from lack of food.... I saw another party of, presumably, kulaks being marched away under an armed guard at Dniepropetrovsk; the little towns and villages seemed just numb and the people in too desperate a condition even actively to resent what had happened."[1]

Communist Party members told Muggeridge that Comrade Stalin was simply doing to the farms what he had done with the factories, and that everything would be fine. But he had questions: "'Are you quite sure,' I wanted to ask 'that the parallel is correct—factories and land? Isn't agriculture somehow more sensitive, lending itself less to statistical treatment? Will people torn up by the roots make things grow, even if you drive them into the fields at the end of a rifle?' It is as impossible, however, to argue against a General Idea as an algebraic formula."[2]

The General Idea of collectivizing farms and farm workers was backed up by propaganda. As urban workers began to starve, films were shown depicting peasants hoarding food. Even the victims in the countryside blamed the kulaks. Muggeridge interviewed one poor peasant who told him life had been much better before the revolution. When asked why there was no bread, just potatoes and millet, he responded, "Bad organisation. They send people from Moscow who know nothing [and] ordered us there to grow vegetables instead of wheat. We didn't know how to grow vegetables, and they couldn't show us. Then we were told that we must put our cows all together and there'd be plenty of milk for our children, but the expert who advised this forgot to provide a cowshed, so we had to put our cows in the sheds of the rich peasants, who, of course, let them starve."

"I thought you'd got rid of all the rich peasants?"

"We did, but their agents remain."

The starvation intensified. People began to die en masse, and some of the survivors turned to cannibalism. The propaganda machine had to print posters saying, "To eat your children is a barbaric act."

By the time the horror was over, at least 3 million people had died from hunger or disease, excluding those executed or exiled. The actual death toll may be much, much higher. It became known in Ukrainian as "Holodomor," which literally means, "The killing by hunger." Because its target was a particular class, some historians and many Ukrainians regard it as an act of genocide.

And Stalin is far from the only self-proclaimed Marxist socialist to have perpetrated such an atrocity. Mao Zedong, who led China to socialist revolution in the 1940s and 50s, attempted in the Cultural Revolution of the 1960s to purge what remained of capitalist and traditionalist thought in the country. Having created a cult of personality with his Little Red Book, Mao and his cronies inspired his young cultists to engage in "class struggle" with his enemies. Millions died or were persecuted.

It is interesting to note the parallels with the Stalinist Holodomor. Mao had collectivized factories and farms in what he called "The Great Leap Forward." The factories produced substandard goods, so much of what little the farms produced was exported to help pay for everything. The result was mass starvation and 30 million dead. The Cultural Revolution came on top of this, with the aim being to dispose of the "counter-revolutionaries" who opposed the leadership's policies. But the targets included those who had helped right the ship after the disaster of the Great Leap Forward.

Those who were said to oppose "Mao Zedong Thought" (remember what Muggeridge said about a General Idea) were said to embody "the four olds"—traditional customs, culture, habits, and ideas. Mao's young cultists formed a "Red Guard" militia that led to the destruction of thousands of years of cultural heritage. Books, artifacts, places of worship, and religion itself were targeted for destruction. Denunciation of counterrevolutionaries was endemic, leading to rape, starvation, suicide, torture, or murder. Minorities such as the Muslim Uyghurs and Tibetan Buddhists were specially targeted.

Because the Chinese authorities still do not allow proper investigation of what happened, death toll estimates from the Cultural Revolution vary wildly, from hundreds of thousands to 20 million. Historians Roderick MacFarquhar and Michael Schoenhals estimate up to 1.5 million deaths in rural China alone, with the same number permanently injured in some way.[3]

And it wasn't just China that suffered the effects of the Cultural Revolution. The Cambodian Khmer Rouge and its leader Pol Pot were highly influenced by Maoist thought (and money) at the time. When they came to power in 1975, they inflicted an even more extreme form of cultural revolution on the country, combining the Great Leap Forward and the Cultural Revolution in one, Year Zero.

Pol Pot had spent many years as a guerrilla leader in rural Cambodia among hill peoples who had seen very few of the benefits of civilization. They lived in a communal fashion, did not use money, and even the national religion of Buddhism held very little interest for them. As leader of the nation he renamed Kampuchea, Pol Pot wanted to bring this way of life, influenced by Marxist and Maoist thought, to the whole country.

Pol Pot visited Mao to seek his advice. Mao told him, "During the transition from the democratic revolution to adopting a socialist path, there exist two possibilities: one is socialism, the other is capitalism," before suggesting that the struggle between the two systems would go on forever. The Khmer Rouge, however, were impatient. According to an American diplomat of the time, the party, "imbued with a Maoist plan to create a pure socialist order in the shortest possible time, recruited extremely young, poor, and envious cadres, instructed them in harsh and brutal methods learned from Stalinist mentors, and used them to destroy physically the cultural underpinnings of the Khmer civilization and to impose a new society through purges, executions, and violence."[4]

Year Zero was an attempt to return Kampuchea, all at once, to the state of agrarian communal living that Pol Pot had idealized in his guerrilla years. The entire population was forced into collectivized work teams, religion was outlawed, and intellectuals (people who knew more than one language, or simply wore glasses) were put in prisons from which few returned. Twenty thousand people were sent to one particularly notorious prison, S-21; only twelve survivors are known. Children were sent from S-21 to the "killing fields," where their brains were bashed in at the Killing Tree.

As a result of the Khmer Rouge's attempt to impose socialism, about 2 million people out of a total population of just under 8 million died. Unlike the Great Leap Forward and the Holodomor, most of these were deliberate executions. Analysis of mass graves suggests about 1.3 million of the dead were executed.

Alas, this might not be the last such story. We may be seeing something similar play out in Venezuela right now. It is well known that the country's economy has collapsed as a result of socialist policies (price controls in particular), but we might be on the verge of something much worse. At the time of writing, stories of incipient mass starvation are beginning to seep out. Cases of malnutrition soared in 2017 as Venezuelans began to complain of the "Maduro Diet" (named after Nicolas Maduro, the president of the country)—a "collective and forced diet" of scavenged food from wild plants and garbage.[5] Studies suggest that during that year six in ten Venezuelans lost weight.

Maduro blames the shortages on an "economic war" waged against Venezuela by America and its allies, and his sympathizers at

Jacobin magazine echo his line.[6] As progressive commentator Jonathan Chait noted of the socialist magazine's coverage of Venezuela, "Demands for more fervent adherence to Marxist dogma have given way to criticisms of the regime's critics."[7]

The lesson is simple: collectivization kills, and attempts to ensure the purity of the system kill more. Yet we don't have to have full collectivization to make people's health worse. Socialization of the medical system can do that.

CHAPTER 11

Socialized Medicine and the NHS

C oming back to Britain, we should recognize that not every aspect of democratic socialist Britain was reformed by Margaret Thatcher. She and her successor John Major privatized most nationalized industries but couldn't shift public opinion enough to affect two pillars of that system. One was the British Broadcasting Corporation, which is not strictly a state-run broadcasting system (if it had been, Mrs. Thatcher would have had more of a chance at reforming it). It is instead state-funded, with every Briton who owns a television set having to fund it by payment of a license fee on pain of criminal penalties.[1] The BBC's outsized influence over British public opinion has made it a thorn in the side of successive Conservative governments. At least it is subject to competition from private broadcasters and Britain's highly competitive media market.

The other nationalized industry that withstood the privatization wave is something most Brits think of as the "envy of the world"—the National Health Service (NHS). Founded in 1948, it offers health care "free at the point of delivery" and is the inspiration for the various "Medicare for All" proposals currently being touted as the inevitable solution to the American health care debate.

The NHS system is far from free, however. It is paid for by the taxpayer. Because of the enormous burden this places on British public finances, the UK actually spends less per head on healthcare than the U.S. spends on publicly financed healthcare alone. When you add in the private insurance many of us have, U.S. spending on healthcare per person is about twice as much as the UK's. Envy of the world?

That, however, doesn't deter the socialist defenders of the NHS on either side of the pond. They say that it's outcomes that are important, and the NHS delivers superior outcomes to the U.S. system, making it tremendous value for the money. They point to health indicators like life expectancy (the UK's is higher), as well as to affordability and efficiency to argue that the UK system is better.

Hold on a minute, though. If we are going to talk about healthcare outcomes, we should actually talk about health care outcomes. Life expectancy in the U.S. is distorted by our high level of gun violence, which has little to do with the healthcare system. If we look at results for care of illnesses, a different picture emerges.

As our friend Kristian Niemietz of London's Institute of Economic Affairs points out, "In a 'blind test', in which we look at health outcome data, and guess which data point represents which country, the UK could easily be mistaken for an Eastern European country. We would certainly never mistake the UK for Switzerland or Belgium."[2] The UK's survival rates for cancer and other chronic illnesses are among the worst in the developed world.

Moreover, non-emergency healthcare is rationed by waiting lists, just as telephones were in the 1970s. The waiting list for a complicated operation can be months or even years long. Emergency rooms are very often overcrowded and lack the number of beds necessary for treatment. A big talking point in the recent UK general elections centered on a picture of a four-year-old boy lying on the floor of an emergency room, supposedly because there was no bed available for him.

Access to medicines is also rationed. New drugs have to go through an approval process just as bureaucratic as the Food and Drug Administration's (FDA), but then also have to be approved as cost-effective by the National Institute for Clinical Excellence ("NICE"). In practice this means that NHS patients are often denied access to life-saving new drugs.

This all makes the talking point about the NHS's value for money less salient. The costs of waiting lists, deaths that occur while waiting, and lack of access to medications are all very real. As Niemietz says, "Any country could keep healthcare spending in check by simply refusing to adopt medical innovation. In more sophisticated estimates of health system efficiency, the NHS ranks, once again, in the bottom third."

It's also important to note that the NHS has become less centrally planned in recent years. It has adopted a "quasi-market" system to try to make up for the lack of the knowledge provided by the price system in real markets. There are even bodies within the NHS that are "dummy" insurers, which Niemietz suggests could form the basis of a privatization leading to a NHS that looked more like the semi-private models of healthcare used in European countries.

None of this is to suggest that the U.S. healthcare system is perfect. It isn't, by any means. But we must recognize that the most socialist system of healthcare adopted by a Western country provides some of the worst healthcare outcomes, at a high per capita cost, and is moving away from central planning.

When it comes to fairness, the NHS is fair only in its provision of equally bad healthcare.

CHAPTER 12

The Bureaucrat

A ll of these terrible things—from orchestrated famines down to delayed hip replacement operations—occur because of a fatal contradiction in socialist ideology. Democratic socialism is supposed to be about democratic control. However, the *demos*—the people—cannot possibly oversee every decision the government takes. Moreover, the socialist democracy is supposed to be about upholding rights, which involves stopping people from doing things as much as making sure things happen. This requires bureaucrats.

The army of bureaucrats necessary to implement socialism lays bare one of the central contradictions of the system. As the British economist Arthur Seldon put it, "The notion that 'society as a whole' can control 'its productive resources' is common in socialist writing but is patently unrealistic. The machinery of social control has never been devised. There is no conceivable way in which the British citizen can control the controllers of 'his' state railway or NHS, except so indirectly that it is in effect inoperative."[1] So socialism is not really rule by the people; it is rule by bureaucrats.

In the socialist commonwealth, the bureaucrat is all important. In a planned economy, it is the bureaucrat that does the planning. In a communist tyranny, it is the bureaucrat who orders the executions.[2] In a democratic socialist country, it is bureaucrats who oversee the nationalized industries and the social services. In a socialized health system, it is bureaucrats who decide when your hip operation will be and which medicines you have access to. The role of democracy in all of this is so limited that, as Seldon implies, it is practically meaningless.

Bureaucrats issue permits and decide who should get them. Bureaucrats preside over everything from life-and-death decisions down to whether or not your public housing is eligible for repairs. In the public health bureaucracies, bureaucrats decide what you can and can't ingest or inhale.

And the bureaucrats are not drawn from the population at random. Some degree of expertise is required, so bureaucrats emerge from training programs administered after selection from (generally) a college-educated pool of applicants. Thus bureaucrats all over the world share two characteristics: they believe what they are doing is for your own good, and that, like the gentlemen in Whitehall, they know better than you.

If bureaucrats were drawn from the people at random, then at least occasionally there would be some who questioned the system. But because people generally aspire to become bureaucrats because they believe in the system, bureaucracy routinely validates itself.

So in the name of equality the socialist system empowers a special class of people to control or at least direct the lives of the majority. Over time, this class becomes entrenched, and has a tendency to become corrupt.

Sometimes the corruption is overt. In socialist India, the bureaucracy became known as the "Permit Raj." In order to do virtually anything, an Indian citizen had to get a permit. The bureaucrats who oversaw these permits knew very well that people would pay to grease the wheel. The former finance minister of India, P. Chidambaram, told PBS, "The most disillusioning aspect of [the Permit Raj] was the rampant corruption in government. Every license, every permit, every amendment was procured by corrupt means."[3]

We should be thankful that in developed countries the corruption is rarely so overt. But a form of unconscious corruption does exist, and it is inherent in the system. Economists call it "public choice."

The theory of public choice is that bureaucrats, as human beings like the rest of us, suffer from an all too human set of incentives. They want to expand their power. They want to grow their budgets. They want to increase the number of staff they direct. And, of course, they want to increase their pay. And because for the most part bureaucrats do not have objective measures like sales by which their performance can be evaluated, they tend to regard these elements as their criteria for success.

I speak from experience. I joined the British civil service after leaving university and was told directly by my first boss, a canny old Scotsman, that increasing your budget and staff were the way to be successful. He proceeded to demonstrate this by doubling his budget and staff within the next two years.

There was no obvious moral failing here. Yet the bill fell on the taxpayer, and my boss, the kindly bureaucrat, was the winner.

One of President Reagan's advisers, William Niskanen, researched this phenomenon in the United States. He found that bureaucrats had a tendency to be "budget maximizers." When cuts *are* imposed, bureaucrats have every incentive to fight back. Gordon Tullock, another academic who studied public choice, found that when the Federal Customs Service had to absorb budget cuts, it fired the front-line inspectors, meaning that the public absorbed far more of the costs, in increased service times, than the Customs Service did.

Moreover, bureaucrats have an incentive to increase their power. When they are granted the authority to make new law through regulation, they tend to exercise this power. When I speak in public about regulation, I often begin with the story of Marty the Magician, who encountered this problem in regard to Casey, the rabbit he pulls from his hat.

Marty was performing one day for an audience of children at the local library in southern Missouri when he was approached by a representative of the U.S. Department of Agriculture flashing a badge. She asked him if he had a license for his rabbit. He didn't, because he had no idea he was required to have one. He got the license but was then told he had to prepare an emergency disaster plan for Casey. The story of why this was all required is a great example of bureaucracy in action.

In the 1960s, Congress passed a law aimed at protecting animals from cruelty. It was a short law, about four pages long. In 1970 it was amended to protect circus animals, giving the U.S. Department of Agriculture (USDA) power to write new regulations, and the agency extended protections to magicians' rabbits and many other "exhibited" animals. Those four pages of law have expanded to fourteen pages of regulation for rabbits alone.

During Hurricane Katrina, many zoo animals were abandoned to die, so the good folks at the USDA required license holders to prepare emergency disaster plans for their animals. Public comments for these rules were overwhelmingly negative, but the rule went through. Marty used a consultant to write a twenty-eight-page plan covering all sorts of disaster scenarios. Another magician from South Carolina hoped one piece of paper would suffice. It simply contained the words, "Note: Take rabbit with you when you leave."

Nevertheless, while it might be possible to reform these regulations, we are probably stuck with something like them. The idea that a law that "protects" animal welfare could be repealed would be laughed down. This is the basis for the super-statutes I mentioned earlier. While people might agree that there are too many laws and too much bureaucracy in this country, each individual law or regulation has its own fervent defenders, who make repeal a heavy lift. The super-statutes have huge numbers defending them. Repealing a super-statute would be the equivalent of a constitutional amendment, in terms of the magnitude of the political battle. So the bureaucrats can generally rest easy, knowing their jobs are secure.

Bureaucrats inevitably make work for themselves, and for the people they have power over. But socialism can take bureaucracy so much further.

CHAPTER 13

George Orwell, Public Choice, and Doublethink

Any student of socialism should take the time to read George Orwell.[1] Two works of his in particular are often read in high schools, and a good thing too. *Animal Farm* and *1984* are excellent reminders that the socialist dream often becomes a nightmare.

Animal Farm is an allegorical tale in which cruelly treated animals rise up against their human masters and set up a society in which "all animals are equal." But one of the pigs who leads the revolt is driven away, the good old work horse is sold to the knacker's yard to allow the pigs to buy whisky, and at the end the pigs appear walking on two legs, with their slogan changed to "all animals are equal but some are more equal than others."

1984 is set in an England ruled by IngSoc, the English Socialist party, which has created a brutal totalitarian state specializing in manipulating the children and the emotions of its citizenry. Its protagonist, Winston Smith, works at the Ministry of Truth, where he changes official history and records to comply with current IngSoc policy. The novel introduces concepts such as "thoughtcrime" and "wrongthink"—crimes committed by simply having thoughts opposed to party policy. The concept of doublethink, the act of holding two contradictory beliefs simultaneously is crucial to IngSoc's control of society. Without it, the state would collapse.

These two novels are biting critiques of socialism in action. They are on point because George Orwell understood public choice. In the words of O'Brien, the villain of *1984*, "The Party seeks power entirely for its own sake. We are not interested in the good of others; we are interested solely in power." That is public choice at its most naked and brutal, but it is still public choice.

Orwell's despair at the effects of actual revolutionary socialism that he had witnessed in the Spanish Civil War and the fight against the Nazis (Orwell recognized fascism for what it was, a variant of socialism) comes through in virtually all his writings. In a semi-favorable review of Hayek's *The Road to Serfdom*, he acknowledged, "It cannot be said too often—at any rate, it is not being said nearly often enough—that collectivism is not inherently democratic, but, on the contrary, gives to a tyrannical minority such powers as the Spanish Inquisitors never dreamed of."

It was doublethink that allowed the collectivist socialists of the 1930s to assert that their oligarchic tyrannies were democratic. Stalin himself proclaimed, "We are for the withering away of the state, and at the same time we stand for the strengthening of the dictatorship, which represents the most powerful and mighty of all forms of the state which have existed up to the present day. The highest development of the power of the state, with the object of preparing the conditions of the withering away of the state: that is the Marxist formula. Is it 'contradictory'? Yes, it is 'contradictory'. But this contradiction is a living thing and wholly reflects the Marxist dialectic."[2]

This doublethink persisted throughout the Soviet era. As I mentioned before, it was a hallmark of socialist tyrannies to proclaim themselves "People's Democratic Republics."

Yet Orwell remained a socialist because he despaired equally of capitalism. In his review of Hayek he noted, "Capitalism leads to dole queues, the scramble for markets, and war," and lamented that "a return to 'free' competition means for the great mass of people a tyranny probably worse, because more irresponsible, than that of the State.... since the vast majority of people would far rather have State regimentation than slumps and unemployment, the drift towards collectivism is bound to continue if popular opinion has any say in the matter."

To Orwell, the sin of collectivist socialism was its promotion of a minority to power and its lack of institutional safeguards for the working man. Socialism had to be egalitarian, and collectivism was not. Interestingly, he regarded the right to bear arms as one safeguard that could work. In a 1941 article for the *Evening Standard*, he wrote, "That rifle hanging on the wall of the working class flat or labourer's cottage is the symbol of democracy. It is our job to see that it stays there."

Whether or not Orwell's view of an egalitarian democratic socialist society underpinned by an armed citizenry is possible given modern socialists' fondness for gun control, it is probable that Orwell himself believed something that we often hear from modern socialists—that "real socialism" hasn't yet been tried. Unfortunately, that's just another example of doublethink.

CHAPTER 14

Has Real Socialism Never Been Tried?

D oublethink, remember, is the ability to hold two contradictory thoughts at the same time. It is doublethink that allows
socialists to believe that actual, real examples of people
attempting to implement socialism, whether revolutionary or democratic, are not real socialism and that real socialism has never been
tried. As a matter of fact, it has been, over and over again—always
with disastrous results.

This brings us back to Kristian Niemietz, who in *Socialism: The
Failed Idea That Never Dies*, looks at the Soviet Union, China, Cuba,
North Korea, Cambodia, Albania, East Germany, and Venezuela, and
examines how each of them began down the road to socialism, developed into a tyranny of a minority, and somehow came to be yet
another example of "not real socialism."

Niemietz describes a three-stage process: First, the honeymoon
period. In this stage, socialist writers, pundits, and philosophers all
wax lyrical about the wonderful new brotherhood of man that is
being created. Democratic control is being exerted over the excesses
of the capitalist system. Plutocrats are punished for their crimes, to

universal acclaim. The initial reallocation of resources and wealth appears to work. The cry goes up that we must follow this example.

Second, the "excuses and whataboutery period." The shine starts to go off the shiny new experiment. The bureaucrats' attempts at planning don't go very well. These failures are blamed on old-regime loyalists or foreign agents working to sabotage the new system. When the injustices suffered by ordinary people are pointed out, the critics are excoriated for cherry-picking, or accused of ignoring the injustices of the capitalist system. As Niemietz says, "There is plenty of whataboutery."

(It should be noted that this stage is where the socialists themselves really go off the rails. Because their General Idea suggests that their policies should be working, the economic failures *must* be caused by counter-revolutionaries or the persistence of old ideas. It is this stage where the kulaks get the blame, or the Four Olds must be eradicated. The deaths turn from accidental to murder. People start disappearing. There are gulags, and there are killing fields.)

Third, the not-real-socialism denouement. By this stage, the socialist intelligentsia worldwide have decided not only is the experiment "not real socialism," it was never real socialism to begin with. Like Winston Smith in the Ministry of Truth, they rewrite the history. In some cases, the facts remain publicly available, but they are ignored and never mentioned in polite company. Suggesting that the experiment was actually real socialism literally becomes *wrongthink*.

Take, for instance, Bhaskar Sunkara's account of Mao and the Cultural Revolution in *The Socialist Manifesto*: "The rhetoric and prestige of [the Chinese Communist Party's] early days, the constant calls to world revolution, made it hard to acknowledge what is now obvious: the CPC's revolution is best understood as a national, authoritarian project, capable of delivering progress at times but far removed from the classic vision of socialism."[1]

In other words, it wasn't real socialism. Wash. Rinse. Repeat.

Pressed to come up with examples of what "real socialism" would look like, today's democratic socialists tend to come up with aspirational paeans to "democracy." As Bhaskar Sunkara puts it, lamenting the failures of previous socialist regimes, "We can also learn that we can't rely on the professed good intentions of socialist leaders: the way to prevent abuses of power is to have a free civil society and robust democratic institutions. This is the only 'socialism' worthy of the name."[2]

The vapidity of this statement should be obvious. "A free civil society and robust democratic institutions" is pretty much Alexander de Tocqueville's description of early American society, a polity that wasn't socialist in the slightest. If socialism is really just democracy and civil society, then America is pretty much already socialist. In which case, what are they complaining about?

In providing more detail on what his ideal socialist society would look like, Sunkara points to Sweden, preferably the Sweden of socialist Prime Minister Olof Palme, around 1976. But Swedes themselves rejected Palme's policies, which, as Swedish economist Johan Norberg points out, "eroded productivity and the long-renowned Scandinavian work ethic."[3] They caused a brain drain of both entrepreneurs and creative artists. Real wages fell as inflation surged. The finance minister during the 1980s later called the policies the Swedes had followed in the 1970s "absurd."

One of the reasons why Swedish labor unions demanded higher wages and inflation resulted is because socialists believe in something called the "Labor Theory of Value." This theory, crudely put, is that things have value because of the labor people put into them. Therefore, if a worker puts many days of hard work into producing something, it must be more valuable than something that requires less work and effort. Even Marx didn't believe the theory in this form, I should stress, but in any form, its validity as a useful economic concept was demolished by something called the "marginal revolution" in economics: it turns out that values are subjective, depending on different individual preferences. Thus a lazy worker has a preference for inactivity over remuneration, and so in a market economy he will be paid less.

This confirms Adam Smith's view that consumers were more important than producers, and that markets should set wage rates. To the socialist believer in the labor theory of value, however, it is the producers who are more important. This disconnect between wages and market value led to the collapse, for instance, of the British car industry, which when nationalized produced shoddy products at high prices.

Swedish voters turned their backs on the labor theory of value and Sunkaranomics in the early 1980s and never looked back. Policies like school choice and free trade have made the country rich again, and despite a large welfare state the country generally ranks as more economically free than the United States.[4] Democratic socialism was democratically rejected.

Sunkara also points to Britain's Labour Party under its current leader Jeremy Corbyn as an inspiration. Corbynism is far more radical than Swedish social democracy, however. His vision for Britain is of just as much central planning as the Britain of Douglas Jay and his ilk, but with a radical social justice agenda on top of that.

Corbyn's election manifesto at the end of 2019 was the most radical since his party's in 1983, which was dubbed "the longest suicide note in history" for its extremist content. It included renationalization of most utilities, rises in the minimum wage, massive public spending on healthcare and housing, a host of giveaways (free broadband, free elder care, free childcare, free prescriptions), as well as promises for a second referendum on Brexit, net zero carbon emissions by the 2030s, and a host of social justice proposals, such as teaching children about the misdeeds and cruelties of the British Empire.

Britain's democracy delivered its verdict on this version of democratic socialism: comprehensive and total rejection outside areas dominated by metropolitan elites. We'll come back to why and how Britain rejected Corbynism so absolutely, but we should note right now that Corbynistas are rejecting the people's decision.

Why is it that democracies reject democratic socialism so often? Occam's Razor suggests it is because socialist policies fail. The socialist, however, has a different answer to this going back as far as Marx: false consciousness.

"False consciousness" is the Marxist term for a way of thinking that stops the thinker from recognizing his true economic and social situation. It's an unfalsifiable knock-down argument for the socialist who can't reconcile his theories with the way people actually behave.

Rural white American who blames a decline in cultural values for his economic predicament? False consciousness.

Young black entrepreneur who thinks he can succeed despite racism? False consciousness.

Proud of the history of the United States? False consciousness.

Swede who thought the 1970s were a bad time for Sweden? False consciousness.

Here are some actual examples published in *The Encyclopedia of Critical Psychology*:

- "People obeying social leaders in the belief they represent god"
- "Working class people believing that certain politicians and policies will benefit the working class when they actually represent and benefit the ruling elite"
- "Believing that society is constructed by autonomous individuals freely negotiating amongst themselves, devoid of power differences and social conditioning"

- And of course: "Believing that capitalism is a democracy that promotes political freedom"[5]

So the democratic rejection of a socialist system isn't actually democratic—*and it can't be, thanks to false consciousness.*

False consciousness is what allows socialist leaders to proclaim that they speak for the People, even when the people reject them. As the German poet Bertolt Brecht put it about a failed uprising in East Germany in 1953, to the democratic socialist sometimes it seems like they must "dissolve the people and elect another."

CHAPTER 15

But Isn't Inequality a Real Problem?

Despite the clear—but unacknowledged—failure of socialism to deliver equality, today's democratic socialists have an egalitarian argument for which they believe they have empirical evidence—that inequality is real, bigger than it has ever been, and rising.

French economist Thomas Piketty became an international superstar when he published *Capital in the Twenty-First Century* in 2013. This tome, which must rival Stephen Hawking's *A Brief History of Time* for the number of books purchased but unread, purports to show that much of the world's increase in wealth has been captured by a small number of capitalists, and will continue to be, resulting in massive and growing inequality. He expresses this as r > g: the rate of return on capital (r) is outpacing economic growth (g). Piketty recommends aggressive progressive taxation at the global level to bring r back down below g.

Piketty's work has become received wisdom among socialists and the progressive left. It's a great argument that something needs to be done about the rise in inequality, which, as *New Yorker* columnist John Cassidy says, has been fueling the revival of interest in socialism: "The legitimacy of the market economy is at stake. From Adam Smith to Milton Friedman, defenders of capitalism have argued that it is ultimately a moral system, because competition ensures that it harnesses selfishness to the common good. But where is the morality in a system where the economic gains are so narrowly shared, and giant companies with substantial market power—the heirs to the trusts—exercise dominion over great swaths of the economy? Until a twenty-first-century Friedman provides a convincing answer to this question, the revival of the S-word will continue." [1]

If Americans care about equality for moral reasons—and they do—rising inequality will continue to inspire them to question a system (capitalism) that appears to promote inequality and to turn to a system (socialism) that promises to reduce it. This is not, as Margaret Thatcher put it, the politics of envy, but rather a deep moral concern for their fellow Americans. To my mind, it is the biggest challenge opponents of socialism have to answer.

The trouble for the socialists is that Piketty is wrong. Not only is he wrong empirically, his description of how inequality is rising (r > g) fails to capture what has really happened, much of which is the result of progressive policies that socialists want to turbocharge. Finally, he fails to ask the right question, which is, *how are the poor actually doing?*

Problems with Piketty's data emerged almost immediately after publication. *Financial Times* journalist Chris Giles found numerous and repeated errors in the data set. Giles, concerned that Piketty's data for Britain seemed at odds with that reported by the Office for National Statistics, took a detailed look at the spreadsheets that Piketty had, admirably, provided for analysis.

Giles found both incorrect formulae and errors in how Piketty had transcribed data from the original source. He also found evidence that some data had been cherry-picked and that others might have been made up. The result was that "once the FT cleaned up and simplified the data, the European numbers do not show any tendency towards rising wealth inequality after 1970."[2]

In response, Piketty and his colleagues Emmanuel Saez and Gabriel Zucman have attempted to create a new data set called the World Inequality Database (WID). These data appear to confirm Piketty's initial findings, showing that the proportion of American wealth held by the top one percent has exploded. These data are cited repeatedly by democratic socialists in the media and on the campaign trail.

Yet, as economists Chris Edwards and Ryan Bourne of the Cato Institute show in a detailed and comprehensive study, the WID data are rife with problems.[3] They depend on tax return data, which are not necessarily a good reflection of wealth. For instance, tax laws change over time, with 401(k)s and healthcare premiums reducing the amount of taxable income reported. Higher divorce and unmarried rates among the poor reduce household taxable income for that group, but not for the wealthier (who tend to remain married—we'll get back to that in Part 4). Most important, tax returns represent only about 60 percent of America's income.

These considerations mean that economists have to adjust the data to get their results. The adjustments made by Piketty, Saez, and Zucman result in the top 1 percent increasing their share of American wealth from 10 percent in 1960 to 15.6 percent in 2015.

Other economists find different results. Gerald Auten of the U.S. Treasury and David Splinter of the Congressional Joint Economic Committee use tax return data to find a modest increase in top 1 percent wealth—from 7.9 percent to 8.5 percent from 1960 to 2015.[4] That's hardly a change that necessitates a complete overhaul of the American economic and political system.

Similarly, Matthew Smith of the U.S. Treasury, Princeton's Owen Zidar, and Eric Zwick of Chicago Booth use Saez and Zucman's data to find a rise in the wealth held by the very top Americans that is about half as much as Saez and Zucman did.[5] They also find that the wealthiest group in aggregate is the top ten percent, but that most of their wealth is tied up in housing, so that they're more like the rest of the population.

Taking these and many other studies into account, Edwards and Bourne conclude that "the estimates from Piketty and colleagues...appear to be incorrect." While the top 1 percent have indeed increased their share of national wealth, the change has not been large, and certainly does not amount to a radical change in differences between Americans.

There are other considerations. Edwards and Bourne also find that most top wealth is "self-made," the result of the sort of entrepreneurship that America has always valued. The founding of Google is a case in point. Sergey Brin (the son of an immigrant) and Larry Page maxed out their credit cards to get the capital to found the company in their garage. Few Americans would begrudge them their success.

Nor have the super-wealthy been raking it in for decades. An investigation into the make-up of the Forbes list of the 400 richest Americans found that just sixty-nine of the rich on the 1982 list remained on the list in 2014, and that includes their heirs, in the cases of those who had died. Those sixty-nine had also seen their fortunes grow more slowly than if they had just made the average return on the stock market during the time. Another study found that the people on the 1987 list grew their fortunes by an average of 2.4 percent. If they had invested in the stock market they would have gained 7 percent.

This reiterates the finding that most of the wealthiest have gotten where they are by adding value to American life. They have produced innovations, founded companies, employed people, saved lives with medical devices, and brought services to previously unserved

markets. They have already "given back" to the community in countless ways.

That's not to say that the rich are always blameless. Far from it.
Yet the most likely reason for bad behavior among the wealthy is not
free market capitalism, but the flip side of public choice—cronyism.

Cronyism and its close associate rent-seeking (where a private
individual or firm looks for an income stream secured by government policy) are creations of government. The crony looks for an
ally in government, most likely a bureaucrat or a politician. The
potential return on investment for fostering a crony relationship can
be vast. As Harvard's Greg Mankiw put it, "The high incomes that
generate anger are those that come from manipulating the system"[6]
Edwards and Bourne enumerate seven different ways in which cronyists can exploit government policy to manipulate the system to
their advantage:

- "Expand sales"—through mandates or subsidies
- "Reduce competition"—by erecting regulatory barriers
  to market entry
- "Tilt playing field"—by instituting unfair advantages
  like "too big to fail" policies
- "Ride the gravy train"—ongoing subsidies allow companies to sit back and coast
- "Escape failure"—getting bailouts that keep companies
  afloat and salaries or payoffs high
- "Hijack benefits"—diverting benefits meant for the poor
  to the crony
- "Get others to pay"—get government to pay for an
  essential part of your business, such as research and
  development (R&D)

Each of these is a source of anger, and rightly so. The "Too Big to Fail" and bailout policies that allowed banks to escape the consequences of their actions during the 2008 financial crisis were the source of egalitarian anger on both the left and the right. Occupy Wall Street and the Tea Party both exploded as the unfairness of the policies hit home. The democratic socialists of Occupy were incensed that poor people lost their homes while bankers got their payoffs. The Tea Partiers were apoplectic that they had to pay for it.

Cronyism and rent-seeking are huge problems and represent corporate sin. What is rarely recognized is that, given the huge returns, there is so little of it. My colleagues Fred Smith and Ryan Young found that corporate welfare amounts to about $100 billion a year, yet corporate lobbying only amounts to $3 billion annually. Why not more?

Fred and Ryan's answer will surprise the Occupier and Tea Partier alike: "Most—but not all!—businessmen, we argue, have a sense of decency or an implicit code of honor that causes them to refrain from rent-seeking behavior, or at least do less of it than one would expect. This virtue defies quantification, which may be why many economists defy incorporating it into their analysis."[7]

In this respect, anger at the cronyists for their behavior is unfair to the vast majority of honest businessmen—including even the super-wealthy. However, as a quotation attributed to French Nobel literature laureate Anatole France puts it, "There are very honest people who do not think that they have had a bargain unless they have cheated a merchant." Our relationship with the merchants in our lives is often antagonistic when it should be cooperative. At the very least, we should recognize that most wealthy people have earned their money and have done so fairly. Again, the presence of a few bad actors does not mean we need to burn the system to the ground, especially when it is within our power to have our elected officials purge the rules that permit cronyist behavior.

Another related issue in the inequality debate that Edwards and Bourne highlight is that over the years governments have made it much more difficult for the average person to grow his wealth. Take Social Security, for example, which is an excellent example of a socialist policy: instead of relying on our private savings or family for our expenses in old age, we have collectivized everyone's retirement in a government program.

All of us who work see around twelve cents for every dollar we earn taken out of our paycheck to pay for Social Security.[8] But Social Security is a tax-funded benefits plan, not a savings scheme. We could have put those twelve cents into investments which not only could grow faster than Social Security's payout levels, they would form a source of capital we could pass on to our children after our deaths.

In economic terms, Social Security *crowds out* private savings. As the non-rich rely much more on Social Security than the rich do, it increases wealth inequality even as it decreases (to some degree) income inequality. The same goes for all sorts of other government programs. As is now becoming apparent, federally provided student loans encourage people to go to high-cost colleges and graduate with debt, meaning that money that they could be putting away for the future goes into Uncle Sam's deep pockets instead.

It used to be that people could save up and invest money in companies instead. Some of us may remember older relatives who lived off their stock dividends. Government policy, much of it inspired by progressive beliefs, has made that more and more difficult. The best investments are limited to people who the Securities and Exchange Commission has declared "accredited investors." To be an accredited investor you must have earned $200,000 ($300,000 for joint income) for the last two years, with expectation that this will continue, or have a net worth of $1 million, not including your principal residence. Accredited investors get access to all the best investment opportunities. It's like having status on an airline, but only if you could afford the first class seats easily anyway.

Government policy has also made sharing in the growth of companies more difficult. When Home Depot went public in the 1980s, it owned only four stores. Its early investors have shared the benefits of the company's fantastic growth since then. These days, thanks to a massively increased compliance burden, most companies don't go public until they are already huge, meaning that the benefits of growth are confined to the company's private investors—another source of inequality.

This is also, by the way, why we see tech companies gobbling up smaller competitors. These days maxing out your credit cards and founding the company in your garage probably won't see you becoming the next Google. The compliance burden of growing your company is such that most business plans include selling out to a tech giant rather than going public. You'll get a nice payoff, but the wealth benefits of your innovation will likely to go to the owners of tech giants rather than to any of your neighbors who might want to invest in your new company. This isn't the tech giants' fault—it's the fault of progressives who pushed through oppressive financial regulation after the crisis (and the earlier Enron scandal).

So if you can't grow your wealth by investing your spare money in companies, where do you put it? The bank offers minimal interest rates, so that's not an attractive proposition. The answer for most of us has been real estate. As zoning laws and other regulations restrict the supply of housing, demand has risen faster than supply. Economics 101 tells us that when that happens, prices rise. Which is great for those of us who have already made the investment, bad for those who haven't.

The result is greater inequality between those who are on the property ladder and those who are not. As noted above, most of the wealth of the top ten percent is secured in housing. And, as we've also seen, that helps foster the resentment that is fueling the rise in the popularity of socialism.

Those supply-side restrictions such as zoning played a major role in the financial crisis of 2008. Everyone knows that the crisis began with a housing bubble. What is less well appreciated is that the housing crisis was not uniform across the country. The areas that did not experience bubbles were those with fewer restrictions on supply. Areas with higher restrictions, in contrast, often employed a regulatory strategy named "growth management," which incorporates policies such as greenbelts, extensive building permitting, targets for urban growth, and "smart growth" (otherwise known as stack 'em and pack 'em high-density urban housing)—in other words, a mild version of centrally planning the housing supply.[9]

Added to this was the role of the Community Reinvestment Act (CRA), another attempt to manipulate market process to achieve the results of central planning. The CRA was based on the idea that social justice demanded greater levels of home ownership among excluded minorities and poor people. Therefore banks were encouraged to lend to these communities, to make loans to a certain number of people who were at or below 80 percent of the median income for a given area. It was such "subprime" loans that led directly to the foreclosure crisis in the areas where house prices had bubbled.[10] As my colleague Michelle Minton found on the eve of the crisis, the CRA had increased the risk to banks while also driving smaller lenders who could not afford the regulatory costs out of the market, concentrating the risk further.[11]

This is not to say that bankers weren't often irresponsible, or that they didn't take advantage of government bailouts to escape personal consequences for their action, dumping the bill on the rest of us, but it is important to recognize one thing. While the financial crisis was a factor in the rise in the popularity of socialism, the financial crisis and the housing inequality that contributed to it were, at least in part, caused by socialist-style planning.

Which brings us back to democracy. Democracy is no surefire antidote to every problem of inequality, and can in fact help create it, deepen it, and perpetuate it. What saves us from the ineptitude of democracy is rights, which we will discuss in the next part.

CHAPTER 16

Radical Equality and Doublethink

When I was growing up in democratic socialist Britain in the mid-seventies, one of the Conservative Party's objections to the way Britain was governed rang true to me. Equality of opportunity was more important than equality of outcome. The Labour Party's policies were all centered around equality of outcome: no one should be privileged enough to have a private education, for instance. Conservatives, on the other hand, proposed policies that would provide gifted poor students with the wherewithal to go to good private schools. That viewpoint won out. Over the last few decades opportunity has generally been agreed to be more important than outcome.

But recently this consensus has broken down. Equality of outcome is now much more important. That's part of the reason why wealth taxes are being seriously advanced as a solution to the inequality problem. Similarly, big firms that deliver huge amounts of consumer value are derided as "too successful."

Yet today's socialists take the argument a step further, proposing a new kind of radical equality based on the demands of social justice.

To the new breed of socialist *any* difference in outcome is a sign of privilege. If men earn higher wages than women, or whites get more loans from banks than blacks, it's an example of the system's being deliberately biased in favor of men and whites. Equality, they contend, demands that this be fixed not just with laws and regulations, but a change in the attitudes of those who are the recipients of privilege. As they put it, being white is like being born on third base and thinking you've hit a triple.

Yet there is classic doublethink involved here. When Asians get better academic results than whites do, it is still whites who are privileged.[1] When large parts of the country are suffering from an opioid epidemic and an explosion of male suicide, there can be no question that these problems should ever be viewed as seriously as, say, whether or not African Americans should be given reparations for their ancestors' slavery.

"Disparate outcome" has become hard-baked into our laws and regulations. Private companies are regularly raked over the coals in the courts for the outcomes of their business practices. Financial regulators, for instance, found that lending practices favored whites over African Americans. The private companies were fined and the bureaucrats started mailing checks to those adversely affected. The trouble was that they had no way of knowing the actual race of people in their database, so they sent out the checks on the basis of the surnames of the recipients. This led to white people receiving checks for having been racially discriminated against.[2]

The doublethink goes farther when it comes to the recent phenomenon of transexual rights. Feminists will argue strongly that female sports stars should be compensated at an equal level to their male equivalents, for example, but are expected to be silent when a clearly biological male enters their sport and wins championships. This doublethink has led to consistent feminists, many of them long-time leaders in their movement, being derided as "TERFs"—"trans-excluding radical feminists"—and being read out of the movement or forced into silence.

For example, the long-time proponent of lesbian rights and multiple Grand Slam–winning tennis star Martina Navratilova, writing in Britain's *Sunday Times* in February 2019, called it "insane" that "hundreds of athletes who have changed gender by declaration and limited hormone treatment have already achieved honors as women that were beyond their capabilities as men."

For this she faced a torrent of criticism, and LGBT groups that she worked with threatened to drop her unless she apologized. She did so, and by June 2019 had made a documentary for the BBC in which she said that trans athletes faced huge challenges, but still maintained the question was "what's the right way to set the rules so that everybody feels like they have a fighting chance?" A sociologist interviewed for the documentary suggested that the only way to resolve the problem was that "a great many sports are going to have to come to terms with the fact they are going to have to mix sports—in other words, dissolve the binary completely and just say they're open."

The doublethink reaches critical levels: equality demands that feminism accepts trans rights, which means that most female sport is going to cease to exist. One can only wait until Title IX comes to this conclusion.

Another example of radical equality and doublethink is that most democratic socialists believe both in privilege and the need for a Universal Basic Income. A UBI, also called a Basic Guaranteed Income, Basic Income Guarantee, or other such formulations, involves the government paying each and every citizen an equal amount of money every year for the privilege of existing. Every citizen, rich or poor, oppressor or oppressed, would receive the same amount, no questions asked, every month.

For instance, Democratic entrepreneur and erstwhile presidential candidate Andrew Yang proposes each citizen over eighteen get $1000 a month. If they already get welfare, they would be given a choice between their means-tested benefits or the open check. This would be paid for by a Value Added Tax on many goods, and (of course) taxes on "big earners" and "pollution."

There may actually be some good reasons for supporting a UBI— if it replaced all welfare programs completely and was small enough not to discourage work it might actually be better than what we have now—but it conflicts with the idea that some people are privileged and deserve less.[3] My suspicion is that if a UBI were to be instituted, the demands for "justice" would quickly result in terms and conditions being applied and larger handouts being given to certain groups. A bureaucracy just as large as the welfare bureaucracy it replaced would be instituted to oversee this.

It would almost certainly be a case of "all Americans are equal, but some are more equal than others." This should be unsurprising. Socialism's claims that it promotes a fair and equal society free from oppression are largely illusory. Where there is equality, it is often the equality of misery, and that misery is usually caused by oppression, violent or otherwise, inflicted in the name of equality.

PART THREE

Does Socialism Free the Individual?

CHAPTER 17

Freedom: The Socialists' Case

"**M**an is born free but everywhere he is in chains." These words are as true now as when Rousseau wrote them in 1762. Unless you are born into privilege, the "freedom" you experience is illusory. For you to obtain the true agency that comes with genuine freedom, there must be a socialist state. This is the only true meaning of "rights."

The average employee, for instance, is nothing but a wage slave. Freedom of contract simply means freedom for the more powerful party to exploit the weaker party. Your employer is your master, and you simply toil on his (for it will be a him) plantation. The right to work, if it means anything, is the right to work under better conditions.

The solidarity of the labor movement is what frees you from this oppression. By combining with other workers to form a labor union, you can balance the power of the employer and negotiate working conditions that free you from this slavery. The right to organize must be recognized and protected in law. Free riders could derail this; therefore, the law must require everyone who is represented by the labor union at the bargaining table—whether a union member or not—to pay union dues. To ensure comparable wages and benefits for everyone, bargaining should be done at the sectoral level, meaning that all those in the same industry abide by the same collective bargaining agreements. Those agreements will require worker representation at all levels of company decision-making, if not outright control (ideally, all workers should be owner-stakeholders).

For those unlucky few who do not have unions to bargain for them, the state must impose a minimum level of worker protections in the form of fair labor standards. Employers should not be able to require long work hours or pay less than a living wage, for example. Vacation should be generous.

The person who is unemployed or unable to work must also be granted the agency to live a free and fulfilling life. So a robust safety net is required, financed by taxation. Unemployment and disability benefits should be freely available and set at a level commensurate with the living wage. To counter the ill effects of unemployment, the socialist state must also provide training for the unemployed and guarantee a public sector job if there are no private ones available.

Freedom also means nothing if you are without a home. The right to housing will be recognized by the socialist state. Landlords will be kept in check by regulations such as rent control, and housing will be kept affordable by the provision of subsidies and government-provided homes, well-maintained at a reasonable rent. Rent support will be available for the unemployed and those unable to work.

Healthcare is also a human right. It is unconscionable to allow profit to be a consideration when people's lives are in question. The state must provide healthcare to everyone regardless of wealth, free at the point of delivery (a socialist will recognize most people will pay some contribution in the form of taxes, with the rich paying the most). The socialist state takes its responsibility for people's health very seriously, so all drugs, medicines, and medical devices must be approved as safe and effective before the healthcare system allows their use.

Education is a human right. The socialist state will provide it, free at the point of delivery, to every child and young adult. Indeed, the government will require all children to receive the same education, to prevent inequality and undue religious influence on youth. The curriculum will reflect the realities of a world of oppression, and so will teach children about current injustices and the evils of the past, inculcating sympathy for racial, sexual, and religious minorities. University education should also be free and available to a much larger percentage of the population than it has ever been. No one should be forced to work when he would rather study for a doctorate in whatever discipline he desires (subject to the requirements of social justice).

To live a free life, a citizen must have access to the right infrastructure. Not just roads, but public transit should be available. Transit should be so good that private vehicles are the exception rather than the rule (this will also benefit the environment). Communications infrastructure should also be available, with the state delivering and maintaining access to broadband internet, for example. Public broadcasting, paid for by taxes, will provide top-quality educational and entertainment programming, available in a variety of formats. Energy will be provided from renewable sources, so that all Americans have a reliable supply of low-priced power. State investment banks will provide the funding to build and maintain this infrastructure.

With these rights guaranteed by a socialist government, people will be genuinely free for the first time. Every kid born into poverty will have the chance to be an academic success. Women will be able to escape abusive relationships and raise families in comfort without the need for a partner. Racial minorities will be freed from the institutional racism that hinders their attainments. The chains of debt and insecurity will be lifted.

By contrast, the "freedom" so beloved of conservative Americans is nothing of the sort. It is the freedom to exploit your fellow man, to insult and belittle people, to endanger them, and to escape the demands of justice. Freedom from tyranny may have been good in 1776, and freedom from slavery good in 1865, but we need much more than that today.

The four freedoms promised by FDR at the time of the New Deal—freedom of speech, freedom of worship, freedom from want, and freedom from fear—have never yet been properly established. Freedom of speech, for example, requires proper community standards to allow people to speak in safety and comfort, while freedom of religion requires a complete separation of church and state, with all the remnants of the old Christian dispensation torn up by the roots—whether it be allowing bakers to claim "freedom of conscience" to be bigoted towards gays or state-owned religious memorials to war dead.

All such relics of the old definition of freedom and rights have to go for Americans to have true freedom. If that means that the Constitution must be torn up and replaced with something else, so be it. True democracy, freed from constitutional restraints, is the only way to guarantee freedoms.

CHAPTER 18

The Individual and the Collective

A s should be apparent, the socialist definition of freedom is very different from the traditional American definition of freedom. Yet the basic language is the same. How can this be?

Socialism and American liberty are, paradoxically, both descended from the same source. Both are grounded in the political revolutions of the eighteenth century. But there is a crucial difference. America was a country born of revolution, but it was a revolution grounded in a view of freedom with ancient roots. Today, political philosophers call this view "classical liberalism."

Classical liberalism is at heart the belief that the individual should be free to determine his or her own destiny. It is tied to what Jefferson termed "the pursuit of happiness" in the Declaration of Independence. This idea goes back to the ancient Greek philosopher Aristotle and his answer to the question, "What makes a good life for a man?" His answer was *eudaemonia*, which is perhaps best translated as "human flourishing."

In the seventeenth and eighteenth centuries, British and American political philosophers viewed the "ancient British constitution" as having been established from time immemorial to secure the right to pursue this good life. They saw much of British history—such as the signing of the Magna Carta—as consisting of struggles to secure this constitution. John Locke and Adam Smith emphasized the important role of property in this conception of liberty.

Meanwhile, a French strand of liberalism had also developed. Philosophers such as Jean-Jacques Rousseau emphasized reason. These thinkers defined freedom in the abstract, as derived from the reasoning of philosophers, rather than from a long history of tradition. In fact, whereas British liberals regarded tradition as vitally important, French liberals were hostile to it.

Nevertheless, the two schools were in strong agreement about the importance of freedom. Thus the Marquis de Lafayette could stand alongside George Washington, and their actions be cheered by Edmund Burke. Alexis de Tocqueville, likewise, was able to examine the institutions of the fledgling American republic with an understanding eye, while Jefferson himself perhaps saw more to admire in French philosophy than in British.

Yet there was a dark aspect to the French brand of liberalism that was not present in the British strand. The French Revolution laid these differences bare for all to see. Legitimate grievances led to a revolution in the name of "*liberté, égalité, fraternité*" ("freedom, equality, brotherhood")—which ended in the imposition of radical equality through the guillotine and the elevation of reason to the status of godhood. Burke stood appalled, Jefferson struggled to defend it, and Lafayette suffered imprisonment and exile.

This early division was reflected in later developments. While it is simplistic to say that the British strand of liberalism resulted in American concepts of freedom and the French in socialism, liberalism did indeed split into two different schools of thought about freedom.

The essential difference revolves around the purpose of freedom. It is what the philosopher Douglas J. Rasmussen, author of works such as *Norms of Liberty*, calls "liberalism's problem."[1]

Classical liberalism—the Anglo-American strain—is based on the belief that the state should be small and confine itself to things such as the common defense and the provision of a justice system for generally acknowledged crimes and peaceful settlement of disputes.

Socialists, on the other hand, believe that the government should require citizens to fall in line with their moral vision for society. Their ideas of justice must be hard-baked into our system of laws. Wage labor, for instance, must be strictly controlled to prevent its lapsing into wage slavery. Labor unions should be the main vehicle for doing this, but laws must constrain those instances where unions are not appropriate, such as family businesses. Thus freedom requires a powerful, if not necessarily large, state that has the capacity to intervene directly to protect freedom wherever it is under threat.

With socialism, freedom can only be maintained by coercion.

It is therefore both ironic and frustrating that the word "liberal" is so often used in America to refer to socialist or progressive policies. Those policies are anything but liberal in the classical understanding of the term.

There is one area, though, where socialists do subscribe to the classical liberal belief that the state must refrain from restricting certain activities. This is the origin of the phrase "keep the government out of the bedroom." Yet socialists are only too happy to snoop around every other room in the house, not to mention the workplace, the vehicles we travel in, and practically every other aspect of our lives. That they do so ostensibly in the name of freedom is infuriating.

If socialists still want to keep government out of the bedroom, they are only too happy to invite it into the bathroom. *Jacobin* magazine, for instance, has campaigned for the abolition of segregated bathrooms. Roger Lancaster, a professor of anthropology at George Mason University, wrote for that periodical, "As a robustly democratic space, unisex toilets would balance public spiritedness—gender equality and equal access—against the need for privacy without reifying gender."

So don't worry; if socialists invade your bathroom, it's simply an expression of democratic solidarity.

To their credit, some socialists recognize the conflict between freedom and the socialist agenda. Good old Bhaskar Sunkara notes in *The Socialist Manifesto* that socialists should avoid "the kind of identity politics that, taken to its extreme, will lead us down the path to a hyper-individualized and anti-solidaristic politics."[2] For these socialists, freedom is all very well, but not if it's a threat to solidarity.

CHAPTER 19

Positive and Negative Rights

N owhere is the language of liberty so confused as in the case of rights. Rights are intimately connected with freedom. Look up "rights" on Wikipedia, and you'll see (presuming some joker hasn't edited it), "Rights are legal, social, or ethical principles of freedom or entitlement." Yet classical liberals and socialists mean very different things by the word.

It was the philosopher Isaiah Berlin who really put his finger on the problem in his 1958 Oxford lecture, "Two Concepts of Liberty." He contrasted positive liberty with negative liberty. My hopeless oversimplification of this fascinating distinction:

- Positive liberty is the freedom to engage in the common government of the polity. It is the liberty of democracy
- Negative liberty is the freedom to be left alone, free from constraint. It is the liberty of the American republic

Berlin noted that positive liberty has been much more subject to abuse than negative liberty. It led to the excesses of the French Revolution and eventually to the Holodomor and the Cultural

Revolution. On the other hand, positive liberty has always played an important part in the true autonomy of individuals.

As well as positive and negative freedom, there are positive rights and there are negative rights.

- Positive rights are the rights to have something provided for you—the right to a job, for instance, or to welfare
- Negative rights are rights not to have something done to you. The right that the government won't interfere with your speech or religion, for instance

It is easy to get these confused. When it comes to the right to bear arms, for instance, we might think that government guarantees us the right to keep a weapon in our home, and that therefore it must be a positive right. That's not the point of the Second Amendment, however, which says, "The right to keep and bear arms shall not be infringed." That's a negative right.

There are positive rights to bear arms around the world. Switzerland, for instance, issues every citizen a rifle and orders him to keep it in his home. The citizens have no choice— the government requires it. There is an argument that the first clause of the Second Amendment, the one about a "well-regulated militia," turns the amendment into a positive right, but that argument has recently been rejected by the courts.

As John Adams, our second president, said before the American Revolution, "Let it be known, that British liberties are not the grants of princes or parliaments, but original rights, conditions of original contracts, coequal with prerogative, and coeval with government; that many of our rights are inherent and essential, agreed on as maxims, and established as preliminaries, even before a parliament existed."[1]

These are the "unalienable rights," "endowed by [our] Creator," that Thomas Jefferson wrote about in the Declaration of Independence. Because they existed before government, they cannot be justly abrogated by government. Any government that tried to do so would be acting tyrannically.

A world of positive rights is sharply different. It is a world where the state is the originator of rights. There are indeed some positive rights that the state legitimately provides. The right to trial by jury, for instance, is something that the state provides and guarantees. Our right to go about our lives in a peaceful society descends from the positive right of the "King's peace," provided to the subjects of Anglo-Saxon kings, a right that has been guaranteed by the people themselves since the American Revolution in the shape of what we call the "police power" of the state.

For socialists, positive rights are a correction of the imbalance caused by some groups' having more power than others. The German Marxist Rosa Luxemburg, an early critic of Soviet-style communism, posited, "Every right of suffrage, like any political right in general, is not to be measured by some sort of abstract scheme of 'justice,' or in terms of any other bourgeois-democratic phrases, but by the social and economic relationships for which it is designed." The freedom to bear arms can therefore be justified if it redresses a power imbalance, say between union striker and bosses' hired thugs. It is no freedom when whites have all the guns and minorities are terrorized by armed police who shoot rather than ask questions, claiming their lives might be in danger. So rights have to be positive rights, to correct these imbalances of power.

Yet positive rights can be a slippery slope. As we saw at the beginning of the chapter, the socialist commonwealth is itself one of many positive rights guaranteed by the state. The more expansive these rights are, the more difficult they are for the state to deliver without requiring something of all citizens. The first step on this slippery slope is taxation—robbing Peter to pay Paul. We are told that this is the "price we pay for living in a civilized society."

Next come limitations on the right to freely contract with other citizens, with requirements such as the minimum wage. Then the government "deputizes" people and businesses, requiring them to deliver the rights supposedly guaranteed by government. We are told that with rights come duties, and that failing to do your duty to the state shows your contempt for the rights of your fellow man.

Expropriation comes next—nationalization of industries, for instance. Not content with your property, governments then interfere with your thoughts. Wrongthink becomes a crime, in the name of protecting the rights of those you think wrongly about. From there it's a short roll down the slippery slope to the gulags and Dzerzhinsky's tears.

Again we see the contradiction in socialism: freedom can only be guaranteed by coercion.

CHAPTER 20

Free Stuff, or Free People?

It's easy to see why positive rights have such an appeal. For many, positive rights are a guarantee of "free stuff." Just look at Jeremy Corbyn's British Labour Party, which guaranteed the following for British citizens in its manifesto during the 2019 election:

- Free college education
- Free wifi on trains
- Free high-speed broadband for every house
- Free social care for people over sixty-five, "with the ambition to extend this provision to all working-age adults" (they didn't even qualify this with "who might need it")
- Free parking at hospitals
- Free annual dental checkups
- Free prescriptions
- Free scholarships to train for "climate" jobs
- Free preschool education
- Free "lifelong entitlement" to skills training[1]

And much more besides, all backed up with positive rights such as an ill-defined "right to food," and giant bureaucracies modeled on the NHS, such as a new National Education Service.

Corbyn was commonly known as the Magic Grandpa for his ability to make promises appear. With this wish list he was more like the Magic Santa. One former Labour MP from the Blair era told Andrew Rawnsley, the chief political commentator for the left-leaning *Observer* newspaper, "Why not throw in free Sky TV? Free iPhones? Netflix and Xboxes all round?"[2] Those were probably kept back for the 2024 manifesto.

Of course, as Milton Friedman kept telling us, there's no such thing as a free lunch. Every time you get a "free" lunch, you pay for it in another way, such as having to listen to a panel on drug pricing policy. Fred Smith, the founder of the Competitive Enterprise Institute (CEI), where I am a fellow, had a rule that no one at CEI could ever call anything "free." We had to use the term "unpriced" instead.

We pay for the "free stuff" guaranteed by these positive rights in a variety of ways, but one peculiar argument has been making its way round socialist thought–circles recently. Socialists have begun to claim we won't have to pay much in terms of increased taxes. Yes, there's always an element of soaking the "super-rich" (defined in the Labour Party manifesto as anyone earning over around $100,000 a year—are you super-rich?), but as anyone who has crunched the numbers knows, there isn't enough money in the wealthiest sections of society to pay for the massive costs of government programs.

Instead, current socialist theory about how to pay for these programs revolves around something called "Modern Monetary Theory" (MMT). The idea is that because governments can print money, they can go into debt (so no need for extra taxation) and then print the money to pay off those debts. Most people will say, "That's crazy!" because they know that previous attempts along these lines have led to rampant inflation.

Socialist enthusiasts for MMT, such as Representative Alexandra Ocasio-Cortez (AOC), however, point to several recent occasions—the Fed during the recent financial crisis, for example—when a government did essentially print huge amounts of money without creating price inflation. They claim that hyper-inflation only occurs when a country can't produce enough to back up the printing, like Germany after World War One, when its industrial capacity had been destroyed.

One of the better-kept secrets of MMT, though, is that for the theory to work, federal jobs in infrastructure construction and the like will have to be at a minimum wage. As we saw in our history of democratic socialism in Britain, unions representing workers for nationalized industries always push for higher wages, which inevitably leads to inflation. Current American law requires that public sector projects use a union "prevailing" wage, so the more public sector projects there are, the greater the inflationary pressure. People who really understand MMT recognize this inescapable fact. It's not clear the politicians do.

The MMT theorists further argue that taxation has a role, but as a deflationary pressure valve. Taxes are used to take money out of the economy, not to provide funds for free stuff. But what this means in practice is that when prices start to rise as inflation begins to appear (especially if this occurs thanks to an external shock like a sudden rise in energy prices caused by instability in the Middle East), politicians will have to raise taxes—at the worst possible time for households. Again, it's not clear whether the socialist fans of MMT understand this.

There are many more issues with MMT, but at heart the problem is this: money is a technology that facilitates the exchange of goods and services. The point of it isn't the slips of green paper you have in your wallet, or the balance in your bank account, but what you can buy with it. As Adam Smith wrote, "Though the wages of the workman are commonly paid to him in money, his real revenue, like that of all other men, consists, not in money, but in the money's worth; not in the metal pieces, but in what can be got for them."

In other words, there are real-world resource constraints on what an economy can do. Sophisticated MMT theorists recognize this, up to a point, but their political fans tend not to. That's why MMT has been lauded as the way to "pay for" the massive cost of the Green New Deal, for instance. MMT is presented as the way America can spend multiple trillions of dollars on new programs without its costing any of us a dime. As Cato Institute monetary scholar George Selgin puts it, it's the Green Land of Cockaigne.[3]

In the real world, the only way to create wealth is to move resources from a lower-valued use to a higher-valued one.[4] When one school kid trades a cupcake to another kid for a juice box, he creates wealth. A government turning on the printing presses does not.

That's why, in the end the source of wealth is free people engaging in free and voluntary exchange, discovering value by that exchange—the very opposite of people provided with free stuff.

CHAPTER 21

Alienation Nation

One aspect of the socialist approach to liberty that doesn't have to do with inflicting misery to guarantee rights relates to a concept essentially invented by Karl Marx: alienation. Alienation is critical to socialist thinking but is a hard concept to grasp.

Marxists.org, for instance, defines alienation as "the transformation of people's own labour into a power which rules them as if by a kind of natural or supra-human law."[1] That's as clear as mud, so I'm afraid we'll have to look at Marx himself (feels like being back in college, eh?) for an explanation of his concept. "What, then, constitutes the alienation of labor? First, the fact that labor is external to the worker, i.e., it does not belong to his intrinsic nature; that in his work, therefore, he does not affirm himself but denies himself, does not feel content but unhappy, does not develop freely his physical and mental energy but mortifies his body and ruins his mind. The worker therefore only feels himself outside his work, and in his work feels outside himself. He feels at home when he is not working, and when he is working he does not feel at home. His labor is therefore not voluntary, but coerced; it is forced labor."[2]

What Marx is saying is that by working to produce something that they have no personal stake in, but which goes on to be sold by their capitalist bosses to people they never meet, workers grow alienated from their "species essence," and therefore from the other human beings around them. As the analogy often puts it, they are just cogs in the machine of capitalism. They are not free men and women.

The alienation theory of labor is therefore very much linked to the labor theory of value we discussed earlier. The thing we produce, the theory goes, is valuable because of the work we put into it—and also, because of that, it has a special value to us. When we come together to create something, we increase that value, and our sense of shared endeavor makes us more valuable to each other. Putting us in a factory not only makes us servants, it is literally soul-destroying.

Interestingly, Marx's description of alienation echoes something said by someone most people would regard as his opposite—Adam Smith. In describing the drudgery of factory work, Smith laments its effects: "The man whose whole life is spent in performing a few simple operations, of which the effects are perhaps always the same, or very nearly the same, has no occasion to exert his understanding or to exercise his invention in finding out expedients for removing difficulties which never occur. He naturally loses, therefore, the habit of such exertion, and generally becomes as stupid and ignorant as it is possible for a human creature to become.... But in every improved and civilized society this is the state into which the labouring poor, that is, the great body of the people, must necessarily fall, unless government takes some pains to prevent it."[3]

Smith and Marx agree that the nature of factory work degrades the individual. Smith, however, contends that the division of labor inherent in the factory process grows the national wealth and therefore enriches us all. Marx, by contrast, argues that all the benefit goes to the capitalist owners of the process.

Smith is surely right on this one. The vast rise in living standards since the Industrial Revolution demonstrates that the rising tide of wealth has indeed lifted all boats. Moreover, there is more to this story than drudgery and exploitation.

Economic historian Deirdre McCloskey calls the explosion in living standards "the Great Fact" that all economic theories must contend with. She contends that this Great Fact was made possible by a novel theory of the dignity of commercial employment.

Both Smith and Marx appear to have reverted to the pre-industrial belief that working for someone else is degrading, even dehumanizing. (Early attempts at an English constitution, for instance, expressly excluded "employees" from the franchise, as they could not be trusted not to slavishly follow their employers' wishes. In law to this day, an employee is a "servant" of a "master," and his situation is distinguished from a partnership of equals, such as a law firm.)

According to McCloskey, however, the Industrial Revolution brought with it a reexamination of virtues and dignity.[4] Both classical and Christian virtues were applied to a life dominated by commerce, so, for instance, justice demanded fair pay and fair work alike, while temperance commanded the growth of savings, and love led to the creation of mutual aid societies.[5] These combined to create a dignity for the employee that had not existed before (and which Smith and Marx both fail to see).

The evidence seems to suggest that McCloskey is right and that the improvement in working conditions seen over the course of the nineteenth and early twentieth centuries was the result of moral decisions in society in general and not revolutionary demand for change. The various "Factory Acts" and the like passed in the United Kingdom, for example, generally happened after most factory owners had stopped employing children, and so on. Henry Ford started paying "six days' pay for five days work" before there were any governmental controls on hours.

Nor was alienation from the products that workers created as big an issue as Marx thought it was. As the economist Joseph Schumpeter noted, "Queen Elizabeth [the first] owned silk stockings. The capitalist achievement does not typically consist in providing more silk stockings for queens but in bringing them within the reach of factory girls in return for steadily decreasing amounts of effort."[6]

With increased wealth came consumer power. The "factory girls" demanded labor-saving devices more than silk stockings. Those devices, also manufactured by factory girls, have freed women and men from domestic drudgery. My grandmother, a coal-miner's wife, had a mangle in her kitchen that she used to wring out wet clothes before hanging them on a line to dry in the wind. She must have spent large portions of her life at such domestic tasks. What Marx viewed as "forced labor" led to the end of such unpaid domestic labor.

Where Marx might have had a point is in alienation from community, although as McCloskey suggests this was mitigated by bourgeois virtues. We'll return to this point in Part 4.

CHAPTER 22

Property Rights and Economic Freedom

S ocialism in its pure form is extremely hostile to the concept of private property. And even its gentler versions, such as social democracy, depend on citizens giving over large parts of their earnings every year to the state for redistribution to other citizens.

A pretty good description of "forced labor" is working but sending your pay to someone who will put you in a cage if you don't do so. That's the way the tax system works for most of us, for a large part of the year.

Thus "Tax Freedom Day." If we paid all our taxes up front every year, we'd start working for ourselves, rather than the government, only when that year's entire tax burden was paid off. In 2019 in the United States, Tax Freedom Day was April 16. Americans essentially spend the first three and a half months of the year in forced labor.

And we actually have it pretty good. In the UK, Tax Freedom Day doesn't come till May 30, meaning Brits work for Boris Johnson five months out of every year. In Germany, it's July 11 before Angela Merkel says thanks. In la belle France, Emmanuel Macron can count you in the ranks of his contributors until July 27, two weeks after Bastille Day.[1]

Yet it's not just expropriation and confiscation that curtail our rights to our property, including the fruits of our labor. Most socialist countries put significant restrictions on what you can do with your property. For instance, Britain still regulates private real estate development in a framework that was designed in the era of democratic socialism in the 1940s. It was part of a program designed to eventually put a stop to all private construction. That socialist dream fizzled out, thankfully, but the planning framework remains. To do virtually any building project—build an addition to your home, for example—you need to apply for "planning permission" and undergo a costly process that allows bureaucrats to decide whether you should be allowed to do what you want with your own property. Thus in Britain land with planning permission already granted sells for a much higher price than land without it.

These regulations infringe on your property rights, which are a core component of economic freedom. That's the freedom to do what you want with your own money, business, and other possessions. Study after study has found that countries with high levels of economic freedom are wealthier, healthier, take better care of the environment, and are just generally better places to live than countries with low levels of economic freedom. At the bottom of all these indices are two sorts of countries—failed states like Afghanistan, and nations like Venezuela, which have sauntered down the road to serfdom by enacting Marxist socialist policies with abandon.

Since 1996, the annual Economic Freedom of the World index, co-published by the Fraser Institute and the Cato Institue, has charted the relationship between economic freedom and indicators of social and economic welfare in countries around the world. The latest edition shows a strong correlation between increased economic freedom and lower infant mortality and poverty. Moreover, both gender and income inequality are at their lowest in the most economically free countries.[2]

Other studies have shown the connection between an entrepreneurial ecosystem and social mobility. For example, the Archbridge Institute found that "factors such as the rule of law, prevalence of corruption, opportunities for innovation, and a dynamic ecosystem for entrepreneurship" are indicators not just of economic freedom but of lowered inequality and increased social mobility. Again, a market system, other things being equal, will produce better results for people's welfare than a non-market system.[3]

Why? A central difference between a Western capitalist economy and a Marxist non-market economy is that the capitalist economies protect economic freedom, to one extent or another, as a human right.

That view is not new, and it is certainly not an invention of modern free market economists. Roman law recognized a sovereign right of property. The first draft of the Declaration of Independence, following the philosopher John Locke, may have named "life, liberty, and property" as inalienable rights. Furthermore, the Virginia Declaration of Rights, which is credited with inspiring some of the language in the Declaration, proclaims, "That all men are by nature equally free and independent, and have certain inherent rights, of which, when they enter into a state of society, they cannot, by any compact, deprive or divest their posterity; namely, the enjoyment of life and liberty, *with the means of acquiring and possessing property,* and pursuing and obtaining happiness and safety."

Of course, one can dispute that. The phrase "property is theft" is a familiar socialist trope. Yet it is not outside the mainstream to say that property rights are human rights and therefore should receive some degree of protection from the vagaries of majority rule, given the long legal and philosophical history of recognizing them.

To some extent (with the major qualification about the tax system discussed above) this battle has seen only one winner over the last century. Expropriation and especially collectivization are now suggested only by the most radical socialists. Yet economic freedom has consistently lost—to regulation.

CHAPTER 23

Regulation, Not Calculation

We've seen that central planning can't possibly produce and distribute goods and services as well as capitalism can because it lacks the myriad information contained in prices set by supply and demand. To address this problem, modern-day socialists have largely abandoned central planning of the economy and switched to regulating businesses.

They say, we will use the market to produce the results we want. So, for example, rather than building twenty-first-century electric Trabants in state factories to reduce emissions, they say to auto manufacturers, make sure that by 2025 the total emissions of your new automobiles are below *a certain level, or face crippling fines.*

Regulation is popular. Most people recoil in horror at the thought of unregulated food or medicine. The idea that our elected representatives should place some controls to ensure health and safety is almost universally accepted. That makes implementing socialism by regulation an elegant strategy. Still, because the regulators cannot take every market factor into account, their attempts to dial the economic knob one way will have other dials turning in other directions.

For instance, in the example given above, the reaction of auto manufacturers was simply to downsize the American fleet. Smaller cars use less fuel, so say goodbye to the station wagon and hello to the compact sedan (and to the gas-guzzling SUV—which, as a light truck, is exempt from the regulations.) The trouble is that smaller cars are less able to withstand accidents, so greater fuel efficiency was achieved at the cost of a higher death toll on the roads. Modern cars have safer "crumple zones," but that makes them more expensive, meaning that some people have to hang on to gas-guzzling death traps for longer. And if you are in an accident, your expensive new car is more likely to be written off.

It's not just businesses and consumers that suffer from regulations. Socialists are increasingly intolerant of personal lifestyle freedom. They want to see less alcohol consumption, less red meat eaten, more miles walked and biked, and so on. Regulation is their preferred tool for doing this (though, to be fair, socialists aren't the only ones pushing these changes.) Again, this can lead to crazy results.

Consider vaping, the new smoke-free habit that looks a lot like smoking. Socialist-lite politicians like Elizabeth Warren want the FDA to crack down on what they describe as an "epidemic" of youth vaping via regulations.[1] Yet teen and adult smoking rates have fallen dramatically since the widespread adoption of vaping products. My wife, for instance, quit smoking after years of trying thanks to the availability of vapes. It's the smoke in cigarettes that is deadly, not the nicotine. So vaping is much healthier than smoking. A regulatory crackdown will almost certainly lead both teen and adult smoking to rise again.[2]

No one is more in favor of regulation as a tool than our green socialist friends (people dubbed "watermelons," because they are green on the outside but Soviet red on the inside). Greens want our whole lives regulated in the name of the environment. They want smart meters to monitor (and eventually control) home energy use. They have destroyed the effectiveness of anything that uses water in the home—showers have no water pressure and dishwashers can't get dishes clean—all by regulations on the manufacture of appliances. They want us to use transit rather than drive, so they use regulations to delay or prevent new road construction and increase the cost of driving. They want most of the United States—including desert areas—to be classified as wetlands to stop development. Name a single human activity, and I can find an environmentalist wanting to restrict it. (That even includes sex—zero population growth has been an environmentalist demand since the start.)

CHAPTER 24

Socialism and the Corporation:
A Love-Hate Relationship

ocialists would rather the traditional American firm did not
exist. Animosity towards the capitalist boss for reaping all the
rewards of his employees' labor, or (perhaps worse) against the
joint stock corporation, where workers don't even know who they're
being exploited by, is a staple of socialist rhetoric. Ideally corporations should be replaced by worker-owned cooperatives or nationalized sectoral industries, but if not, they'll be strictly controlled
through regulation, and their owners and stockholders taxed to
oblivion.

Margaret Thatcher called this "the politics of envy." Her message
that it was sinful successfully countered the idea that profit is about
greed and turned the British Labour Party from a democratic socialist party to a social democracy party for over two decades.

But now the politics of envy is back in a big way. Not only are
corporations accused of greed, they are alleged to be destroying the
planet. New-style businesses like Uber are accused of not just exploiting workers but outright cheating them. Yet increasingly socialists,
realizing the political impossibility of getting rid of the corporations,
are turning to co-opting them instead.

Corporations grow up because entrepreneurs need to find investors to help finance their businesses. In addition, to keep transaction costs low, they need to hire employees rather than contract for each individual routine transaction. That's the foundation of the corporate structure of owners, management, and workers.

For the past century, that structure has been under attack by socialist activists, who have long viewed corporations as ideological battlegrounds, with management arrayed against workers. You will probably notice there a shift in target from Marx: management is the enemy, not the ownership. In fact, much of the Naderite-era attack on corporations was based on the idea that corporate management did not act in the stockholder owners' interest.

Ironically, however, the National Labor Relations Act and similar New Deal laws set the corporate structure in stone, in the name of "protecting" workers against management. Certain aspects of the employment relationship were guaranteed by government enforcement—including overtime, unemployment insurance, paid time off, opportunity for union representation, and other requirements on employers. This required a corporate form of business.

Before the modern corporation, economies were characterized by what Adam Smith called "the system of natural liberty," where businesses were small in scale and owners invested their personal assets into the venture and freely contracted with other businesses and individuals for services.

This model lost out to the corporation because of what are called transaction costs related to identifying and contracting with other businesses to perform a service for you. It was far easier and more reliable to directly employ someone to do the job, even when required to offer the protections imposed by law. That's why the corporation survived for most of the last century despite the increased costs of hiring.

Corporations also reduced transaction costs within their own organizations—and the prospect of internal strife among workers—by devising innovative new business arrangements. The franchising business model turned many workers into potential owners. New management models turned other workers into junior managers. The "us versus them" model that created labor strife broke down, and union representation in the private sector plummeted.

But in recent years the costs of contracting with another party have been coming down. In some sectors of the economy, corporations are being replaced by networks or platforms that enable two-sided markets, where the purchaser of a service can buy it from a small-scale supplier rather than a large corporation. The most famous example is Uber, which provides a network matching riders to drivers, so they don't have to go through a taxicab firm. And despite having some corporate features, Uber is a very different animal from a taxicab company.

Given the left's hatred of corporations, you'd think that socialists would cheer this development. Not so. Instead, many view Uber as exploitive—perhaps even more so than a 1930s-era corporation, because it deprives workers of New Deal–era legal protections based around the corporation.

Previously, workers who set their own hours and had significant control over the way they worked were regarded as independent contractors, free from the requirements of much of employment law. But now California, through its AB5 law, is leading the way in redefining contractors as employees. So the woman who goes on a ride-sharing app to earn some extra income driving passengers while caring for a sick relative is no longer an independent contractor, but an employee of the app firm. Understandably, companies affected by this law are cutting workers.

During the Obama administration, there was a rash of attempts to make corporations more liable for employees, for example to change overtime rules to eliminate huge swathes of junior management positions—something that would have interfered with the aspirations of ambitious young workers (employers would probably cut back on or even eliminate overtime opportunities.)

The National Labor Relations Board ruled that franchisor companies are "joint employers" of their franchisees' workers, making them responsible for day-to-day matters like individual workplace conditions and working hours—a burden that would make franchising a much less attractive business model for companies seeking to expand.

While both these regulatory expansions were changed under the Trump administration, they are still very much in the playbook of the labor union movement, and Democrats in Congress are trying to make them law. Paradoxically, this suite of policies actually reinforces the old corporate structure that was set in place in the 1930s. The result will be more large corporations based on an "us versus them" paradigm that pits management against workers—in other words, the very corporate structure socialists claim to hate.

There are two reasons that socialists want to see this structure continue. First, it gives government agencies immense power over employment conditions. Second, large corporations are easier to unionize than smaller companies. And the dues paid by employees for union representation—which they may not even want—makes large corporations a huge source of funds for political campaigns.

Corporations know this. The political and cultural attacks on them have helped lead some of them down the road to "woke capitalism," which we'll discuss in the next part. The politics of envy may end up not destroying the corporation, but making it a vehicle for socialism. It's a good bet that Marx didn't see that one coming.

CHAPTER 25

Free Speech and the Socialist Commonwealth

I f you're a democratic socialist you must believe in free speech, surely? Free speech is a cornerstone of democracy, no?

In actuality, while the socialists of the sixties and seventies may have been at the forefront of the "Free Speech Movement," that's far from the case today.

As we have seen, for the socialist, rights are doled out by the government in order to correct power imbalances. Free speech, then, may be important so that leftists can "speak truth to power." But it has its limits. And once the socialists are the power, those limits can be very strict.

Socialists disagree on the proper limits of free speech. Marx condemned both censorship and the liberal idea of free speech. The socialists who have come after him reflect his doublethink. Herbert Marcuse, for instance, the German-American philosopher often regarded as a guru of the "New Left," regarded tolerance as a tool deployed by capitalists to exploit the working class (which Marcuse regarded as hopelessly passive and seduced by advertising), and so he argued for suppressing the free speech of conservatives and capitalists.

This Marcusian view informs the current debates about free speech. The left now wants to put intellectuals—professors and students—in charge of which messages people should be exposed to. Anyone who might deliver a message seen as justifying or defending the current system of class, race, and gender exploitation must be shut up. An academic such as Charles Murray (no relation) is as much to be denied a platform as a provocateur such as Milo Yiannopoulos.

Then there are the mandatory "trigger warnings" like the (tongue-in-cheek) one at the start of this book. Classic works of classical literature are now "problematic" because they may contain non-disapproving references to slavery.

Trigger warnings are therefore a great example of the intolerance that Marcuse recommended. They limit people's exposure to the ideas of classical thinkers. Leftists on campus claim that they are simply "warnings," which students are free to ignore, but they have the effect of reassuring the student that they do not have to engage with ideas that challenge the left. Thus they represent what psychologist Jonathan Haidt and Greg Lukianoff, president of the Foundation for Individual Rights in Education, call the "coddling of the American mind" in their book by that title.

And many socialists also espouse this Marcusian suppression of alternative views even outside the campus. Green environmentalists, for instance, have led a decades-long and surprisingly successful campaign to suppress the views of anyone opposed to the radical restructuring of the economy in the name of the climate.

Their argument is nominally about science, but the climate debate is about far more than climate science. There are several questions in play, and some of those questions are certainly scientific. Those include whether or not the world is warming (it is), whether or not mankind's actions have anything to do with it (they do), how sensitive the climate is to those actions (a hotly debated scientific issue), how various scenarios will play out (a contentious area given the implausibility of extreme scenarios), and how those scenarios compare to the actual data we have (quite poorly).

Yet even if we conclude (or assume) that there is indeed a significant and immediate problem caused by greenhouse gas emissions, science has very little to tell us about the best way to solve it. We could, for instance, massively reduce greenhouse gas emissions by keeping the developing world in poverty. Or we could deindustrialize the West and revert to a medieval lifestyle. Both solutions would kill millions of people and lead to massive hardship for the rest. Both are valid approaches according to the science. It is economics that tells us what is actually feasible.

Moreover, there are geopolitical questions as well. It is well known that China has said that it will cut emissions—starting in 2050. Does the U.S. have an obligation to pay for climate "damage," when the rest of the world has benefitted considerably from innovations literally fueled by U.S. emissions? These are questions of geopolitics, and science can make no more than a small contribution to the discussion.

All of these matters should be subjects of significant public debate, yet to express doubts about the economic feasibility of the Green New Deal, for instance, is to open oneself up to the accusation of being a "science denier." Socialist environmentalists, seeing science as a trump card to play in achieving the radical transformation of the economy they want, have managed to suppress debate that might undermine their position. This campaign has been so successful that major newspapers and broadcast media no longer ascribe to journalistic norms of seeking the other viewpoint, for fear of being castigated for enabling "denialism."

The result is a Marcusian suppression of conservative and free market voices on a matter of profound political importance. One side is portrayed as being open-minded, pro-science, and concerned

about the future, while the other is suppressed for being willing pol-
luters, shills for oppressors, anti-science, and pro-extinction. It isn't
exactly a fair fight.

This model has been so successful that it is being exported to
other areas. When there was a wave of illnesses and deaths from the
use of black-market THC-vaping products, campaigners against
e-cigarettes saw their chance. They worked with allies in the public
health bureaucracies to portray e-cigarettes in general as dangerous.
The line was that if you are in favor of e-cigarettes, you're in favor of
teen smoking (the exact opposite is true), and no one should listen
to you. Within a few months the Trump administration had been
pressured into banning flavored vape products which have been
shown to help adults quit smoking, and Congress had raised the age
for buying any tobacco products to twenty-one. Both free speech and
the freedom to smoke were victims of this campaign.

To be fair, not all socialists espouse suppressing the speech of
their opponents. Socialists like *Jacobin's* Samuel Farber, for example,
believe that they must counter the arguments of those who seek to
persuade people against socialism with socialist arguments—rather
than by shutting down their opponents' free speech. Farber is
opposed to trigger warnings because they encourage "a climate of
undue caution, timidity, and even fear in what should be a wide-
ranging but mutually respectful exploration of ideas." He believes
that trigger warnings are the result of "neoliberalism" and the "view
of higher education as consumption in which tuition dollars are supposed to buy a pleasurable product."

But even Farber's defense of free speech has its limits. He views
picketing and heckling as free speech that can counter the speech
of "persuaders," ignoring the reality of the "heckler's veto," that can
prevent a Charles Murray from speaking by shouting him down.
And he believes that other speech—such as campaign speech from

groups like Citizens United—should be regulated. Farber points to Rosa Luxemburg's argument that rights are all about economic power relations.[1]

This underlines the fact that where socialists respect free speech, they do so only as a positive right, one that must be strictly controlled and regulated by government for the good of all. When you really examine the socialist argument for free speech, it is not motivated by any desire for liberty as liberty—and that also goes for every other right socialists claim to support. Freedom is only good insofar as it advances equality. Socialists may use the language of freedom, but they reject liberty as a value.

CHAPTER 26

Liberty for Its Own Sake—and for Our Health

C lassical liberals value liberty for its own sake. This is what the Founders meant when they talked about "unalienable" rights. We have freedoms because we are human beings, not because the government awards them to us to redress economic or power disparities. We don't lose rights simply because we are rich (nor do we gain them because we are poor).

That is why it's time to fight back against the idea that we must sacrifice liberty to redress egalitarian grievances. The current debate over healthcare is a case in point. Under Obamacare, in order to ensure that people don't go uninsured, the rest of us have to pay more. So that those with pre-existing conditions can switch plans easily, the rest of us have to put up with higher deductibles. In order to ensure that young women have access to unpriced contraception, Catholic nuns have to pay for a healthcare plan that includes it. The way the debate is going, the socialist ideal of single payer healthcare looks more and more attractive.

It's time to say no, the value we place on liberty demands a different approach. That does not mean that we do not care about the plight of the uninsured, people with pre-existing conditions, or young women. But to preserve our freedom, solutions to these problems should be met within a voluntary framework.

We actually have exactly such a framework in our history. The basis of insurance itself is the voluntary mutualization of risk. Americans came together to form mutual aid societies to provide their members with things like funeral expenses, assistance in times of trouble, and, yes, access to healthcare. Wherever you see a "Shriners' Hospital" or similar institution, it was built by a mutual aid society. Mutual aid societies routinely negotiated healthcare fees that were far lower than the prices currently negotiated by insurance companies.

Moreover, mutual aid societies were that socialist ideal—member-owned cooperatives. Officers of the society were elected, and very often they came from vastly different social classes. An unschooled treasurer of a local chapter could learn financial management skills in his role—skills that were transferable, enabling him to move up the ladder in his job. Membership in one local chapter could easily be transferred to another chapter through a national framework, providing a member with an immediate social network should he move from one city or state to another, thereby ensuring a more mobile society.

Not only does liberty have its own rewards, it also complements the egalitarian value. Liberty fosters equality. But that is not the only value of freedom or the only good it fosters. Liberty to engage in family life, neighborliness, and mutual aid—Burke's "little platoons" of civil society, which tended to be crowded out by the government in the shape of mutual aid, also complement the value of community and tradition that we'll discuss in the next chapter.

Ironically, some thinkers who are often associated with socialism, such as the anarchist Pierre-Joseph Proudhon, who coined the phrase "property is theft," were strong proponents of mutual aid as the basis of socialist society.[1] It is a discredit to our modern-day socialists that this voluntarist line of thinking, which recognized the value of liberty for its own sake, has been sidelined in modern socialist thought.

Modern socialists have huge problems with mutual aid. They worry that mutual aid societies could be exclusionary, reinforcing power differentials through racism, sexism, cisgenderism, and so on. Historically, mutual aid societies demanded that their members meet certain standards, such as sobriety, and those standards were often informed by religious principles. In essence, they practiced preventive care. While it seems obvious that most forms of modern mutual aid would include contraception in preventive care, the idea that some might not and promote abstinence instead would be seen as a breach of the positive right to contraception.

Breaking the link between health insurance and employment would also reduce the power the government has over the corporation. According to the Kaiser Family Foundation, the average corporation spends over $20,000 per household on health insurance—up 54 percent over the last decade (if you wondered where your pay raises were over the last ten years, there's your answer).[2] Essentially, the government has forced private employers to pay for its expansion of health insurance.

Finally, mutual aid would reduce the power of bureaucrats. Decisions would be made in negotiations between patients and providers, not by bureaucrats. Anyone who wanted to could build a new medical facility; if it wasn't deemed necessary by the community, it would simply go out of business. There would be no need for bureaucrats to issue a "certificate of need," as many states require. Competition would flourish, driving prices down.

Healthcare is just one issue where the voluntary principles of liberty are being driven out of our public discourse by the revived rhetoric of socialism. Banking is another area. Community banks and the mutual societies that are credit unions have been a major casualty of the push for more regulation following the banking crisis of 2007–08. The big banks that were most at fault during the crisis were able to afford the burden of compliance. Smaller banks couldn't. They merged or closed in record numbers. Others, like the State National Bank of Big Spring, Texas, simply ceased making mortgage loans to their customers, who were generally low-income people purchasing low-cost properties.[3] Complaints about the power of banks led to some of the most disadvantaged bank customers' suffering the most.

Socialists use the language of freedom, but a close examination of their aims reveals how hostile they are to the value of freedom. Where socialism allows freedom, it does so on the basis of dictating what you are allowed to do with that freedom. Socialist freedom is no freedom at all.

PART FOUR

Can Socialism Sustain Communities?

CHAPTER 27

The Socialists' Case

Socialism is the only way to preserve what is important to us. Society is always at the mercy of predatory capitalists, who strip-mine it to make themselves richer. They do not care about our jobs, our careers, the opportunities for our children.

The capitalists are the true revolutionaries, in the pejorative sense of that word. Motivated by a desire for profit, they dissolve "all fixed, fast-frozen relations, with their train of ancient and venerable prejudices and opinions," as Marx said. Nothing is safe from their unrelenting search for new markets to exploit, assets to seize, and people to use and cast aside.

The heart of socialism, by contrast, is a strong labor movement, protected and privileged by law, which provides good jobs and protects careers. Moreover, in a truly socialist society you will finally have democratic control over the capitalists. They won't be able to close down the factory where you work and force you to move across the country to find a new job just to make themselves richer.

Because a socialist society will eliminate poverty, it will also reduce crime. No one will be motivated to rob his comrades.

The brotherhood that socialism embodies will ensure that violence of all sorts—personal and corporate—is minimized. A socialist world will be a virtuous world.

We'll also have a healthier society because we will have democratic control over the firms that push unhealthy foods and lifestyle choices on us, not to mention all having cradle-to-grave free healthcare. Your children will grow up healthier and safer.

Speaking of your children, you can be certain that they will get a good education. Socialism will provide top-quality free education from preschool to postgraduate level. Our elders, meanwhile, will also rest easy as they will receive top quality, free elder care—and they will be able to retire earlier too, with a state-guaranteed pension to ensure they can continue to live in comfort.

Nothing is more at risk from the depredations of capitalists than our environment itself. The lakes, the forests, the purple mountains, and fruited plains of America are all targets for their rapaciousness. Even the very air we breathe is polluted by their greed, whether it be with particulate matter from the fuels they foist on us or from the global warming that is making species die and our weather descend into chaos.

CHAPTER 28

Socialism and the Divine

Y ou'll remember that when I sketched out the socialist position on freedom I mentioned freedom of worship. Freedom of worship is not only a fundamental American liberty, but also very much part of our tradition. Not for nothing is it called "America's first freedom." Long before there was a Constitution, our ancestors came here to pursue freedom of worship. And while their ideas of religious liberty were both limited and very different from ours, they started an evolving tradition of increasing freedom of conscience, which helped America avoid the religious strife other Western nations suffered.[1]

Socialists' attitude toward religion has also evolved. Early utopian socialists took religion as the basis for their beliefs. Marx, however, famously denigrated religion, calling it the "opiate of the masses," and saying, "Religion is the sigh of the oppressed creature, the heart of a heartless world, and the soul of soulless conditions.... The abolition of religion as the illusory happiness of the people is the demand for their real happiness."[2] Marx may not have disparaged religion entirely, but Lenin took the ball and ran with it, saying, "Atheism is a natural and inseparable part of Marxism, of the theory and practice of

scientific socialism," although he declined to make atheism a requirement of Communist Party membership.[3]

Atheism was part and parcel of the Cultural Revolution in China
and Year Zero in Cambodia (in those countries, Buddhism and Islam
were the main targets). Yet in other countries socialist revolutionaries tied themselves to the Cross or to Islam. In Latin America a whole
new brand of Roman Catholic theology evolved to reconcile socialism with the Church—Liberation Theology (the current Pope, Francis, has strong links to this strain of Catholicism,which centers on a
"preferential option for the poor" and tends to portray Christ as a
revolutionary figure.[4])

In short, modern socialism has an ambivalent relationship with
religion, especially organized religion. According to the statistical
analysts at FiveThirtyEight (working from a survey conducted by the
Public Religion Research Institute), Americans who are not religious
"are 10 percent more socialist, on average, than religious Americans,"
with the gap greater among older people than young (young people
are more likely not to be religious regardless of politics).[5] Not being
religious is also strongly correlated with the distinguishing features
of the democratic socialists we have met—young, college educated,
childless, living alone.

On the other hand, many of the poor and working-class con-
stituencies that socialists court are much more religious. African-
American churches, for instance, have been major organizational
forces in liberal politics for generations. Hispanic immigrants also
tend to take religion seriously. Even white women are more religious
than white men, according to most polls.

This puts socialists in a bind. Attacking religion itself is likely to
put off people they need to attract. So modern American socialists
tend to concentrate on one way to square this circle: the aggressive
pursuit of separation of church and state.

Any separationist worth his salt will bend over backwards to say that all he wants to do is to ensure that the First Amendment's strictures on religion are respected. State establishment of religion, he will contend, includes any attempt to prefer one religion over another, or over none at all. Thus it is fine to pray in school, but not fine for teachers or other school authorities lead a prayer, or ask a student to do so. The courts have accepted this argument. As David French notes, "In a series of shocking Supreme Court cases, a progressive court elite destroyed the Protestant public school and ruthlessly disentangled Protestant church and state. School prayers? Gone. Daily Bible reading? Gone. Recitations of the Lord's Prayer? Gone. Prohibitions on teaching evolution? Gone. The Ten Commandments on school walls? Nope, no longer. In a roughly twenty-year span, the edifice of America's Christian public educational establishment was nuked from orbit."[6]

Many Americans, even religious ones, accept this now, though it was hotly debated when the courts were on their march through the classroom. Some teachers and school administrators, fearful of falling afoul of the new rules went further, essentially chilling religious activity among students at school.

But even that wasn't enough. Separationists waged war against the dead, objecting to state-owned memorials in the shape of crosses. They attacked the unborn, challenging laws that attempted to protect babies in their mothers' wombs as religiously inspired attacks on women's right to choose. The laws are always depicted as the last step on the way to imposing the theocratic society depicted in *The Handmaid's Tale*, with young women reduced to servitude as nothing more than vessels to carry their masters' children.

The latest wave of attacks is on small business owners who attempt to live their faith through their business. By means of "equal opportunity" jurisprudence and "public accommodation" laws, separationists sue business owners in an attempt to force them to bake cakes or arrange flowers for weddings whose validity the business owners do not recognize.

These laws were passed with good intentions, but something has gone badly wrong. Culture and tradition can give those who don't fit in very bad experiences. A gay person's life can be made a living hell by those who do not approve of his lifestyle. It is right that state or federal law attempts to prevent this from happening. As law professor Michael Greve has pointed out, the reason we have a federal government in the first place is to prevent local tyranny.[7]

But the live-and-let-live spirit of these laws is clearly being perverted by the separationists—to punish people of whose lifestyle *they* disapprove, all the while claiming that *they* are the victims. In the age of social media, they have a mob at their command, which can be activated by the use of a single hashtag. In days past, a gay boy might have found himself the victim of mob violence. Now a Christian baker might find herself the victim of "doxing," with a dangerous crowd trespassing to threaten her in her own home.

The aggressive use of separation-of-church-and-state tactics is functionally the state promotion of atheism. It delegitimizes faith and drives it underground. And the religious communities who are the targets of socialist organizers are being played for fools. African-American pastors and Latino priests may be the last to be targeted, but they will be targeted.

In a socialist America, therefore, religion will almost certainly be drummed out of the public square. Politicians will not—unlike every previous generation of American politicians—appeal to religious morality. They'll have to turn to something else instead.

CHAPTER 29

How Socialism Discourages Virtuous Behavior

Religion has been the traditional lodestar of society, but socialists propose that socialism itself should play that role. People will be motivated towards virtuous behavior by the love of their brother man and the recognition that their brothers will be there to help them in their own needs.

Marx is very clear on this. He deprecates "moralism" as the imposition of some external code, but promotes an ethics that leads to one of his most famous phrases (in a great example of his purplest prose): "In a higher phase of communist society, after the enslaving subordination of the individual to the division of labour, has vanished; after labour has become not only a means of life but life's prime want; after the productive forces have also increased with the all-round development of the individual, and all the springs of co-operative wealth flow more abundantly—only then can the narrow horizon of bourgeois right be crossed in its entirety and society inscribe on its banner: From each according to his ability, to each according to his needs!"[1]

What does this mean? It means that in a highly developed socialist society (which Marx called communism), talented people would be so filled with brotherly love that they would happily work to aid their less talented, more needy brothers and sisters. The socialist state would arrange the distribution of wealth arising from this happy state of affairs.

If there is a hierarchy of socialist societies, it is based on this principle. At the lowest level, the social democracy, a welfare system is in place to arrange the redistribution of wealth earned in the private sector. At the next level, democratic socialism, many people work for the state in nationalized industries according to central plans, with welfare provided from the presumed surplus of that planned economy. In the highest level, communism, everything is planned, and everything is perfect, with only the truly unlucky needing to be recipients of welfare that arises organically from the perfect economy.

It never works out that way. Social democracies find that welfare discourages the potentially needy from working according to their abilities. Democratic socialist states discover that workers in nationalized industries want more of the state's resources dedicated to them. And the only real attempts at communism turned into oligarchies or dictatorships so quickly that no one had time to notice that those with abilities were being imprisoned or executed.

The demoralizing effect of welfare is easy to understand. While few people disagree with the idea of a safety net for those who through no fault of their own find themselves unable to work (even Friedrich Hayek thought there should be one), welfare payments for disabilities that are easy to claim but hard to prove will make people more likely to claim them.

Social scientist Nicholas Eberstadt has tracked the rise of disability claims in the United States.[2] In 1960, there were 134 working for every man of working age registered as disabled. By 2010, the ratio had plummeted to sixteen to one. He also found that during that time claims for muscular-skeletal disability and mental disabilities (two diagnoses easy to make but hard to prove) had increased significantly.

The result was a new lifestyle—men of working age sitting on the couch playing video games. While Eberstadt admits that it is hard to prove that welfare *caused* this lifestyle, it certainly financed it. Another of Eberstadt's findings is that men who enter this lifestyle rarely leave it. Welfare appears to be discouraging the virtuous behavior of work. As Eberstadt put it, "The progressive detachment of so many adult American men from regular paid labor can only result in lower living standards, greater economic disparities and slower economic growth than we might otherwise expect. And the consequences are not just economic. The male exodus from work also undermines the traditional family dynamic, casting men into the role of dependents and encouraging sloth, idleness and vices perhaps more insidious."[3]

And America is not alone. Even the supposedly successful Nordic welfare states found it difficult to deal with long-term unemployment during the 1990s. They solved their problem by changing whom the recipient of the welfare was to be. In Sweden, for example, welfare reforms included increasing incentives to work through wage subsidies. Employers who found it difficult to pay people a living wage in a world of strict labor regulations and high taxes on work were granted wage subsidies to make up the difference. This helped reduce long-term unemployment rates but amounts to a giant money-go-round. Subsidies could clearly be less if welfare were not so generous.

Meanwhile, America has seen a sharp drop in the number of long-term unemployed without resorting to such measures. The better economic environment of the last few years has resulted in record low African-American male unemployment. Long-term unemployment is now below the level it was before the financial crisis.[4] We will need to await the results of the 2020 census before we can see if disability claims have decreased. If they have, that will suggest that the hope of opportunity can beat the certainty of welfare.

We have already seen how labor unions in social democratic Britain demanded ever-increasing slices of the national pie, even if it meant the dead went unburied. A popular joke in Britain in the 1960s and 70s had union officials saying, "I'm all right, Jack," an expression of an extreme degree of selfishness. From each according to his abilities, to each according to his greed, it might be said.

When we hear about the importance of a strong labor movement to democratic socialism we should remember how the labor movement actually works. To begin with, thanks to FDR's National Labor Relations Act, unions take money out of the pockets of workers— *whether they belong to the union or not*. The logic for this legalized larceny is that the NLRA grants a union exclusive power to bargain with the company in its bargaining unit. If non-members were able not to pay union dues, the theory goes, they would become free riders, and the union would be too ill-funded to do its job, strengthening the hand of company bosses.

What forced union dues do, in reality, is strengthen the hand of union bosses in their interests. The way this actually works was laid bare in the recent *Janus v. American Federation of State, County, and Municipal Employees* case at the Supreme Court. The Court found that the unions concerned had used Mark Janus' dues to finance not only bargaining over wages and benefits, but also a political agenda that he did not support. As Mr. Janus was a government employee, this amounted to forced political speech. That's a no-no under the First Amendment. As a result, government labor unions can no longer extract dues from non-members.

In private sector unions, too, the union bosses enjoy a lavish lifestyle and salary while promoting their own political agendas with dues paid by the workers that their unions represent. That includes lobbying for policies that are often harmful to society at large.

Take, for instance, the Jones Act, a bill requiring that goods shipped by water within the United States must be shipped on American-built, -owned, and -operated ships. It is supported by a large number of labor unions, including the International Longshore and Warehouse Union, the Marine Engineers Beneficial Association, the Inland Boatmen's Union, and the Sailors' Union of the Pacific. They do so on the basis that it "protects American jobs."

What the Jones Act actually does is increase the cost of ships, the cost of labor on those ships, and the cost of goods transported on those ships. It costs every one of us. Moreover, as the rule applies to aid as well as trade, it increases the cost of disaster relief efforts. New Orleans after Katrina and Puerto Rico after recent hurricanes have been hurt by the Jones Act, and administrations regularly have to suspend it when the outcry starts to mount after a disaster. Furthermore, the Jones Act has demonstrably not protected American jobs. The American merchant marine fleet is now down to around 200 ships, with about 2000 laborers supported at ports. An International Trade Commission report found that repealing the Act would cost only thirty-six jobs in the shipbuilding industry. All this comes with a price tag of $2.8 billion a year. Yet the political clout of labor unions has made repealing the act essentially impossible. Labor unions simply do not act out of consideration for the community at large.

We should also look at the role labor unions have played in the destruction of major American industries. The pension agreements they made with large automobile companies in the middle of the last century, for instance, became such a huge burden that the banking crisis of 2008–09 wrecked the industry, with bastions of American business such as General Motors dependent on government support.

While Detroit was built on American ingenuity and know-how, it was devastated by intransigent labor unions. The United Automobile Workers laid the groundwork alongside Jimmy Hoffa's Teamsters in the 1930s, and the labor activists declared, "Let's make Detroit a Union Town!" They succeeded. Even after foreign car manufacturers like Volkswagen or Toyota realized that they should build their factories in states that had a "right to work" opt out from certain parts of the NLRA, Detroit continued to unionize workers, especially in government. In 2012, it was discovered that the Detroit Water & Sewer Department had a farrier on its payroll—someone paid to put horseshoes on horses' feet—at the union rate of $56,000 a year including benefits.[5] The job description was last updated in 1967.

"I'm all right, Jack" appears to be an international creed. Indeed, union leaders often talk about standing up for the rights of workers internationally. The recent U.S.–Mexico–Canada trade agreement, for instance, was highjacked at the last second by labor union interests, who insisted on inserting various provisions aimed at securing rights for workers in Mexico's automobile industry. In fact, the likely effect of these provisions is to ensure fewer jobs for Mexicans and higher prices for American consumers. What the union leaders really celebrated, however, was the creation of a new international enforcement regime. That's part of a pattern of socialist thinking.

CHAPTER 30

Transnationalism and Nationalism

In 1864, French and British labor activists founded the First International, an attempt to coordinate the activities of a variety of socialist, communist, anarchist, and labor organizations around the world. It failed owing to squabbles between Marxists and anarchists led by Mikhail Bakunin. Anarchists were excluded from the Second International, founded in 1899. This body collapsed following the First World War, after which socialists around the world were divided between the creation of the Soviet Union and the Communist International and what would eventually become the Socialist International, today's coalition of democratic socialist parties.

The vision of international socialist brotherhood pervades the socialist movement. The socialist anthem, *The Internationale*, looks forward to the day when socialism will unite humanity as one:

'Tis the final conflict;
Let each stand in his place.
The International working class
Shall be the human race![1]

◆   ◆   ◆

Socialism has therefore always had an international complexion to it. In recent years, however, partly because of the constant squabbling and schisms that have dogged the international groups, socialists have become more transnationalist than internationalist

Let me explain what I mean by this. Internationalism entails nationalism, by which I mean the recognition of the nation state as the fundamental constitutional unit of world governance. This idea goes back to the Treaty of Westphalia in 1648. Nations negotiate with nations as sovereigns, recognizing them as equals regardless of size, and, in the words of the United Nations charter, agreeing that "nothing should authorize intervention in matters essentially within the domestic jurisdiction of any state." Socialist internationalism accepted those premises.

Transnationalists, however, want to establish a different international order. As John Fonte of the Hudson Institute explained in his 2002 essay identifying and defining "transnational progressivism": "Transnational advocates argue that globalization requires some form of transnational 'global governance' because they believe that the nation-state and the idea of national citizenship are ill suited to deal with the global problems of the future."[2]

Transnationalists want to subjugate national governments to the dictates of global governance through a series of treaties and transnational organizations that have powers, if not to intervene in the domestic jurisdiction of a state, to request and even require state action.

The European Union, for instance, requires that member states implement its legal directives. The International Criminal Court can issue arrest warrants for war crimes suspects in member states, allowing for politically motivated investigations. The United Nations Convention on the Law of the Sea (otherwise known as the Law of the

Sea Treaty) socializes the resources of the deep sea and instructs member states exploiting those resources to pay developing nations, even landlocked ones, for the privilege (the Treaty was designed in Soviet times, to provide income streams for Soviet satellite nations.)

Socialists back transnational bodies such as the International Labor Organization (ILO). The ILO, founded by the League of Nations after WWI, was heavily influenced by the Second International and by American union leader Samuel Gompers (although America did not formally join until the New Deal). The body became part of the United Nations after WWII, and Soviet attempts to influence the body turned it into a political football. The United States withdrew from the ILO for a few years in the late 1970s over the body's recognition of the Palestinian Liberation Organization, returning in time to influence it in favor of recognizing the anti-communist strikes in 1980s Poland. While it has advanced many admirable causes, such as the fight against forced labor, the ILO is also in favor of a host of harmful labor regulations, including the minimum wage.

The ILO and many similar organizations are currently toothless thanks either to U.S. non-participation or to U.S. opposition to their interventionist tendencies. That could change under a socialist administration. As *Nation* editor Katrina vanden Heuvel wrote in the *Washington Post* in December 2018, "Senator [Bernie] Sanders has joined with former Greek [socialist] finance minister Yanis Varoufakis to issue a more sweeping call for a new progressive international movement. It would work to unite progressives around the globe and to redefine global institutions such as the International Monetary Fund, the World Bank, the International Labor Organization and the United Nations to further shared prosperity rather than enforce austerity, and to address the "massive global inequality that exists, not only in wealth but in political power.""

The good thing is that making these bodies more powerful by transferring sovereignty would almost certainly require treaty-making, and the treaties would have to be ratified by two thirds of the U.S. Senate.[3] We therefore have a constitutional bulwark against transnationalism. However, the history of the United Kingdom's involvement with the European Union shows that once the process starts, it can be very difficult to unravel.

Yet that constitutional defense is vulnerable to end runs. The Obama administration realized that its consent to the Paris climate treaty would face an uphill battle for ratification. Therefore the administration announced that the treaty wasn't actually a treaty at all, but an "executive agreement," which didn't need the advice and consent of the Senate. We can expect any socialist administration to negotiate a slew of such executive agreements. The good thing about an executive agreement is that an incoming executive can repudiate it, as President Trump did with Paris, although that might have been more difficult if the drafters of the agreement had made withdrawal harder.

As Paris showed, the current push for transnationalism comes in the form of environmental policy, which is increasingly the future of socialism.

CHAPTER 31

Watermelon Environmentalism

Nowhere has socialism taken such a grip as in conservation. America is a land of plenty, with stunning natural riches and a veritable treasury of the earth's bounty. It is a true American value to want to conserve these fruits for our children and future generations. That value has been claimed as its own by the green environmental movement, to the exclusion of all others. And that movement has become dominated by activists who see socialism as the only way to preserve the environment.

Again, America is not alone in this change. "Green" parties grew up in many Western countries in the 70s and 80s as a "third way" of politics, opposed to both capitalism and socialism. But in recent years those parties have steadily adopted more socialist policies, and now increasingly represent the hard left in Europe. The reason for this wholesale adoption of socialist orthodoxy is the reduction of environmental politics to one issue: climate change.

Climate change is the perfect excuse for socialism. It stipulates that capitalist economic activity imposes increasing costs on all of us that are not captured in the price system ("externalities") and that therefore capitalist activity must be severely constrained by democratic means to prevent these costs turning into catastrophe. Economic activity must first be regulated, then controlled. Because science tells us what level of carbon dioxide in the atmosphere is acceptable, planners must work on that figure as the basis for all economic activity henceforth. Our entire energy and transportation infrastructure must be rethought, with mass deployment of renewable energy–generating facilities and severe restrictions on the use of private motor vehicles. This must be done on an accelerated time line and can therefore only be done by the use of state capacity (government power, to the rest of us.) Private industry, and especially capitalists, cannot be trusted to provide any answers at all in this arena. But this restructuring can provide and sustain millions of new jobs. Ideally, this revolution should be coordinated at the global level, with transnational authorities guiding and overseeing the process.

This is why the environmental movement across the West is pushing national variants of a "Green New Deal" or a "Green Industrial Revolution." The American version, as proposed by Representative Alexandria Ocasio-Cortez and Senator Ed Markey, for instance, contains a long list of environmental policies, such as

- Replacing all fossil fuel–reliant energy generation with zero emission sources (but not nuclear power)
- Eliminating "pollution and greenhouse gas emissions from the transportation sector as much as is technologically feasible," including by building high-speed rail links
- "[U]pgrading all existing buildings in the United States and building new buildings to achieve maximal energy efficiency, water efficiency, safety, affordability, comfort, and durability, including through electrification"

- Reducing all fossil fuel use in manufacturing and industry as much as is "technologically feasible."
- Removing pollution and greenhouse gas emissions from farming (cows, as is often noted, are significant producers of methane, a greenhouse gas)
- Restoring and protecting fragile ecosystems
- Cleaning up hazardous waste and abandoned sites
- Promoting international technology transfer

But it doesn't stop at these environmental policies. It includes a lot more besides (this is the "New Deal" part of "Green New Deal"):

- Public-funded infrastructure banks
- Vague-sounding policies that could be the basis for climate-related welfare
- National training and education programs
- Publicly financed and directed research and development
- Democratically controlled investment and planning
- All jobs created by the plan to be "high-paying union jobs"
- "Guaranteeing a job with a family-sustaining wage, adequate family and medical leave, paid vacations, and retirement security to all people of the United States"
- Provisions aimed at unionizing all jobs in the nation
- Strengthening existing labor, employment, and discrimination law
- Autarkic trade policy including carbon tariffs at the border
- Privileges for indigenous people
- Strengthened antitrust law
- "Providing all people of the United States" with:
  - High-quality health care
  - Affordable, safe, and adequate housing

- Economic security
- Access to clean water, clean air, healthy and affordable food, and nature."[1]

This is a program for imposing socialism on the United States. But the central planning is hidden. Bureaucrats will have a field day, and the individual will be subjugated to the collective—because if he isn't, the planet will die. This demonstrates why environmentalists are often called "watermelons." They are green on the outside, but a deep, bloody red inside.

It should go without saying that this watermelon program will cost a fortune. My colleagues Kent Lassman and Daniel Turner analyzed the costs of just the environmental parts of the plan— energy generation, transportation, building retrofits, and so forth. (They couldn't find enough information to estimate the costs of the agricultural provisions). In the typical state, the Green New Deal "would cost a typical household more than $70,000 in the first year of implementation, approximately $45,000 for each of the next four years, and more than $37,000 each year thereafter." The median household income for 2019 was $75,500. The effects would be devastating.

Yet those costs are just a fraction of potential total costs, once you include the more Marxist policies. Take, for example, the cost of education and retraining. There being no detail, it is difficult to know how to assess this goal. The city-state of Singapore, with a population of 5 million, is spending around $1 billion a year on retraining, allowing every Singaporean aged twenty-five or older a credit of around $350 to spend on approved retraining courses.[2] It will be much more expensive to administer such a program in a population sixty-five times larger and much more geographically dispersed.

The applicability of retraining must also be taken into consideration. In Youngstown, Ohio, displaced steel workers signed up for training in refrigeration and computer repair, but there were no jobs in refrigeration, and the computer training was rendered obsolete by technological change.[3] It would require something close to omniscience to provide universally effective job training. What we do know is that the previous attempt to provide something similar, in the original New Deal, was an ignominious failure.[4]

A federal jobs guarantee is also fraught with problems. Subsidized or guaranteed jobs "crowd out" jobs created by the market, simply replacing existing jobs. The vast bureaucracy that would be required to administer such a regime will be subject to enormous public choice problems, as the bureaucrats pursue their own advantage at the expense of the people they are supposed to help. We should remember that the Paris Commune, which guaranteed a job to all citizens, was reduced to having gangs of workers dig holes and other gangs fill them in.

I could go on. The Green New Deal would go much further in socializing the entire economy than any western social democracy currently does, or even any democratic socialist state did in the past. It would be truly revolutionary.

Perhaps a revolution would be in order if there were a genuine planetary emergency and the policies would significantly ameliorate the crisis. But the Green New Deal fails on both counts.

As my colleague Marlo Lewis has demonstrated repeatedly over the years, claims that the world is about to end are overblown, based on "unreliable climate models, inflated emission scenarios, political hype, and unjustified pessimism about human adaptive capabilities." Most of the claims about what will happen in the future are based on climate models that assume a massive increase in coal power, when in fact coal has been declining as a global fuel source and will continue to do so. They also use a "sensitivity" factor for how the atmosphere reacts that is out of kilter with the consensus of recent research. While hurricanes and wildfires hit the headlines, the evidence is clear that people are suffering less now from extreme weather events than they did in the past.[5] That's because we adapt, and the free market system has made us much more resilient to weather disasters. We don't need to propitiate the sky gods anymore.

Moreover, the economic policies being proposed in the Green New Deal *just won't work*. They never have. Centrally planned economies perform much less well, to put it mildly, than free economies. As the emissions problem (if there is one) is a global problem, crippling America's economy will do very little to solve it as long as developing nations, especially China, continue to emit ever-larger amounts of gases—as the current global agreements allow them to do.

As for the New Deal policies of the plan, their likely effect will be to make us much poorer than we would have been and thereby less resilient to natural disasters. Moreover, if we are to build huge amounts of green infrastructure quickly, that will mean no environmental impact statements and the loss of huge areas of wildlife habitat. The Green New Deal makes no sense on its own terms—unless there is a planetary emergency, and there isn't.

Yet as I said, Green parties are riding high right now across Europe. They have effectively replaced the old socialist parties in much of the continent. Because they have the virtue of an idealism that cannot be ascribed to socialist parties whose ideas and policies have failed repeatedly, they will continue to be the vehicle that brings these even more radical policies to the forefront of political debate. It says something that the figurehead for this movement that ostensibly seeks to preserve the world for future generations is a sixteen-year-old girl with the policies of Rosa Luxemburg. If you want a vision of the future, imagine being lectured by Greta Thunberg—forever.

CHAPTER 32

How Regulation and Taxation Create Carnage

T here is one issue where American traditionalists are growing increasingly sympathetic to socialism, even if they don't immediately recognize it as such. This is the vexed problem of what to do about the areas of the country that are being left behind as other areas go from economic strength to economic strength. This is the country of J. D. Vance's *Hillbilly Elegy*, the areas of the country where President Trump in his inaugural address said there had been carnage: forgotten America.

The traditionalist might very well agree with the socialist diagnosis, which would go something like this: forgotten America is the victim, first and foremost, of capitalism. Capitalists imposed a neoliberal winner-takes-all regime that undermines community and traditional values. They opened up America to the forces of globalization in the name of "free trade," while at the same time breaking down the protections workers had enjoyed through their labor unions. Their policies led to the decimation of America's manufacturing base and the disappearance of "good jobs"—blue collar jobs with the security of a living wage and a job for life. Moreover, bankers and their ilk made owning a home more expensive, the profit motive pushed up the cost of a college education, and private healthcare businesses made falling ill ruinous. The result is that young Americans in forgotten America can't afford to get out, while their parents dread the day the neoliberal axe comes for their job and worry that their children will be the first American generation to have a worse standard of living than their parents.

It's a damning indictment, and one to which socialists claim to have the answers. Strict controls on capitalism, including breaking up big soulless companies, the replacement of free trade with managed trade that ensures jobs won't go overseas, strong labor unions, restrictions on banks, free college education, and free healthcare—all policies pushed by democratic socialists—would solve the problem. Communities would flourish once again, and Americans could pursue the American Dream, free of anxiety.

The socialist temptation is obvious. Socialism claims to be better for American values than capitalism is, and the socialists appear appears to have the evidence to back up that claim. Who are you going to believe, neoliberals or your lyin' eyes? The experience of many Americans seems to support the socialist diagnosis, and that makes them more susceptible to the temptation.

Thus we can have the spectacle of conservative warrior Tucker Carlson praising Senator Elizabeth Warren's "economic patriotism." Her diagnosis will prod many conservatives to nod in agreement:

> These "American" companies show only one real loyalty: to the short-term interests of their shareholders, a third of whom are foreign investors. If they can close up an American factory and ship jobs overseas to save a nickel, that's exactly what they will do—abandoning loyal American workers and hollowing out American cities along the way.

Politicians love to say they care about American jobs. But for decades, those same politicians have cited free market principles" and refused to intervene in markets on behalf of American workers. And of course, they ignore those same supposed principles and intervene regularly to protect the interests of multinational corporations and international capital.

The result? Millions of good jobs lost overseas and a generation of stagnant wages, growing inequality, and sluggish economic growth.

The trouble is that this diagnosis is incorrect. The great economist Frédéric Bastiat noted that in economics there are two effects, the seen and unseen. What we tend to do in politics is try to deal with the seen effects, and ignore the unseen, which may be much more important. What has happened in forgotten America is only partly economic, and this diagnosis ignores the cultural aspects. While the unseen aspects of the economic problem are much more complicated than the simplistic picture of Wall Street or Silicon Valley plutocrats throwing American workers on the scrap heap.

Let's look at the question of manufacturing and "shipping jobs overseas" first. The figures all show that we're actually at an all-time high in manufacturing output, having finally recovered from the great recession. What has dropped is the number of manufacturing jobs. That's not because of "shipping jobs overseas," but because of innovation. From the 1980s to the great recession, innovation led to vastly increased productivity per worker—a company needed far fewer workers to generate $1 million in output in real terms in 2005 than it did in 1980. In turn, those workers are paid more. The average manufacturing worker earns $87,000 annually today—and the average *household* income is $75,500. That's far more than a living wage.

Moreover, when we look at job "churn" in the U.S.—the number of jobs lost compared with the number created, we find that trade ("shipping jobs overseas") accounts for only a small percentage—15 percent—of the jobs lost every year. If we are concerned about factories closing and jobs lost, we should recognize that the reason is one of the great strengths of the American economy: innovation.

This phenomenon is why the economist Joseph Schumpeter coined the term "creative destruction." Just because a job is destroyed does not mean things are terrible. The loss of that job opens up new opportunities. Where have all the switchboard operators and typists gone? In the vast majority of cases, on to better things.

Yet clearly not all job destruction is creative. The stories of factories closing and wrecking a community are legion. What stops the destruction from being creative? The answer is regulation and taxation. Our failure to grow roses from the ashes of a factory closure is a failure of *adaptation*, not the inevitable result of "vulture capitalism."

America has become a difficult place to start a business, where historically it has been one of the easiest. We have made it hard to get start-up capital. We make it difficult to hire people. We make it costly to rent facilities and power them. We have also made it hard to grow a business because the more people you employ, the more bureaucratic hoops you have to jump through and the more extra costs you have to take on.

The result has been a collapse in what economists call "dynamism." That's the process by which new firms take over from old firms, small firms become big firms, and jobs are created to replace those destroyed. Young high-growth firms are a major source of job creation. Yet dynamism has been in decline for several decades, with firm exits overtaking firm creations for the first time during the great recession.

Such a decline obviously has many causes, but the rise of the regulatory state is clearly one of them, in my opinion probably the most important. If regulations make it more difficult for a bank to lend, the aspiring entrepreneur who has been laid off from a factory job will be left out in the cold. This might also be one reason why certain parts of the country have recovered and other have not. Venture capitalists have filled the breach by investing in many startups, but they are well known for not investing outside certain areas (such as California or Boston), and they don't pay much attention to, say, people who want to start a plumbing business.

Talking of plumbing, most states require you to possess a state license to work as a plumber—Idaho has six different categories of plumbing licenses. Obtaining a license takes time (thousands of hours of training), costs money, and in most states you have to pass an exam. Plumbing is just one example of a profession where occupational licensing is the rule. Others include cosmetology, hair braiding, and even flower arranging, each with its own training requirements.

Occupational licensing is an obvious barrier to people's retraining for a new profession after being laid off, and thus it makes for less entrepreneurial activity and less dynamism. Even if you got a redundancy settlement from your previous employer, you probably don't want to have to spend it all on two years' retraining (including classes) before you can open your florist shop.

Let's suppose you do get financial backing from somewhere (say you have a well-off aunt), manage to get your occupational license (perhaps your aunt is on the licensing board), and open your business—well, you might then find that your troubles are just beginning.

When you hire you first employee, there are a host of regulations you have to comply with. With your fourth, even more. With the fifteenth, the ball really starts rolling. More regulations pile on at twenty, twenty-five, fifty, and a hundred employees. Moreover, there are regulations that apply depending on how many hours an employee works. Obamacare famously kicks in once an employee works over thirty hours a week.

The predictable result is that there are a lot of businesses with three, or nineteen, or forty-nine employees. And many limit employees to less than thirty hours. But even these figures don't account for the businesses and jobs that are not created as a result of regulation—an example of the unseen effects of the regulatory regime.

Senator Warren is missing the point by a country mile. Conservative politicians have not defended free market principles and failed to "intervene" to help the American worker. If anything, they have stood by, or even aided, as Warren and her ilk have passed law after law that delegates power to regulatory agencies that have heaped these burdens on entrepreneurs. What America needs is more of a free market, not less. The problem that the forgotten Americans are facing is not free markets run amok, but the collapse of civil society.

CHAPTER 33

Business and Civil Society

"Civil society" is a term of art among economists and cultural researchers. Essentially, it means an ordered society without much in the way of government intervention. Look it up on Google, and you'll find the definition, "society considered as a community of citizens linked by common interests and collective activity."

Civil society was what Alexis de Tocqueville was writing about in *Democracy in America*. He famously noted, "Americans of all ages, all conditions, all minds constantly unite. Not only do they have commercial and industrial associations in which all take part, but they also have a thousand other kinds: religious, moral, grave, futile, very general and very particular, immense and very small; Americans use associations to give fêtes, to found seminaries, to build inns, to raise churches, to distribute books, to send missionaries to the antipodes; in this manner they create hospitals, prisons, schools. Finally, if it is a question of bringing to light a truth or developing a sentiment with the support of a great example, they associate."[1]

This was still true until comparatively recently. Tocqueville contrasted American associations with how things were organized in

France. There, he noted, it would be the state taking the lead instead. In England, a landowner or lord would take the lead. This made American civil society unique.

Mutual societies, we have seen—Elks, Oddfellows, Rotarians— were examples of civil society in action. The churches were another nucleus of civil society. Organized sports grew up as people came together to play games for exercise and social life, and then formed leagues. If you still have a bowling league, you are engaging in civil society. When government schools crowded out association-created schools in the Progressive Era, civil society responded by creating parent–teacher associations.

Business exists alongside civil society and is often intimately connected with it. As the University of Chicago's Edward Shils noted, "A market economy is the appropriate pattern of the economic life of a civil society."[2] Credit unions and thrift organizations arose as answers to the question of how to save and invest. Businesses can sponsor activities of civil society. Some associations grew up among employees of one particular workplace. The wages paid by employers helped fund their workers' associations. Businesses gained a good name by aiding associations, and associations found business a willing partner in their activities. When we think about the ideal small-town America that has become the forgotten America, we are remembering a world in which civil society was strong. As my friend Tim Carney, an editor at the *Washington Examiner*, puts it, "America is the land of opportunity because America is the land of civil society."

Finally, civil society was distinguished by being, well, *civil*. Politeness and manners, showing respect for other members of society, were extremely important. Associations promoted the arts and letters and the pursuit of scientific knowledge. Respect for property was extremely important, as property rights underpinned the existence of civil society free from the state.

Socialists, however, *hate* civil society.³ I do not use that word lightly. Here's an example from Roland Boer, a professor at a Chinese university: "Many assume that 'civil society' is a neutral term, meaning the realm of human activity outside the state and outside the economy. However, the term is far from neutral…. [W]hat 'civil society' really means is bourgeois civil society. It is inescapably tied up with the development of capitalism and the seizure of power by the bourgeoisie."⁴

For the socialist, civil society embodies and empowers the exploitation of the working class by the bourgeoisie and their capitalist enablers. This is because of our old friend alienation, in this case alienation of the worker from the state. It is the state, representative of and democratically controlled by the worker, that should play the role played by civil society. When he was mayor in the 1980s, Senator Bernie Sanders told a stunned audience at a United Way fundraising event in Burlington, Vermont, that he didn't think private charities should exist.

Alienation is certainly present in forgotten America, but it is an alienation of a different sort. In 2018 Tim Carney wrote a book called *Alienated America,* in which he sought to answer the question why certain communities had backed Donald Trump in the 2016 election, while others had supported his main primary challenger, Senator Ted Cruz. Carney found that those areas that had supported Trump were areas where civil society had collapsed. People had become alienated—not from their labor, but from each other.

One of Carney's most interesting findings was that the average Trump voter was actually doing quite well, and had followed the "success ladder"—finished high school, got a job, got married, had children *in that order.* It was their neighbors who had not and were floundering. These voters' support for President Trump seemed to echo concern for their neighbors. But they were not likely to have tried to remedy the problem by engaging in civil society themselves.

By contrast, areas that supported Senator Cruz were much more likely to have active civil society associations, most likely centered around churches or religious traditions. These voters were actively involved in helping their neighbors.

What caused the alienation and the demise of civil society? Carney suggests that big business may have had something to do with it. Closure of local businesses and their replacement with big box stores or internet retail deprived communities of "third places" where people would meet and interact with their neighbors. Yet Oostburg, Wisconsin, one of Carney's case studies, has a Walmart superstore just ten minutes' drive away, and it was still a healthy community. I speculate, but it may be that areas with strong civil society are resistant to the negative effects of big business. More important to my mind, Tim points to the absence of strong faith communities in forgotten America.[5]

Coming back to Nick Eberstadt's work, these are also the places with high rates of unmarried men, who are much more likely to be out of the workforce and on disability than their married contemporaries.[6] In these areas, Carney finds that people live like they think the upper class lives—unmarried, behind gates, oblivious to tradition. This is an example of what Carney calls "the Lena Dunham fallacy." In fact, the upper class are likely to be married, heavily involved in their communities, and, in all aspects except their politics, bourgeois in their behavior.[7]

As my colleague Richard Morrison puts it, "Middle- and upper-class Americans have not been corrupted by the progressive, free-love legacy of the 1960s, but they have been coopted by its non-judgmentalism. The people who now constitute the economic and professional elite—most of whom are highly educated and left-leaning—are either unable or unwilling to share the good news of the good life with their poorer neighbors. The most successful Americans live according to what most people would consider old-fashioned values, but refuse to preach what they practice."[8]

The besetting sin of today's bourgeoisie is that it practices traditional American community values but insists that government take care of everyone else. Thus the current ruling class has progressively eliminated the role of civil society from education (government schools), helping the less fortunate (welfare), banking (regulations favoring banks over credit unions), sports (applying antitrust law to sports leagues), and even the basic community building block of marriage (attacking the idea that marriage is a good thing through a variety of laws and regulations), all in the name of ending inequities.[9] Regulations even mean that those areas where civil society endures are often more responsive to government than to their members (think about how your Home Owners' Association has become more bureaucratic over the years).

Socialism would not just keep this dynamic going but intensify it. As we've seen, existing religious institutions would come under yet more attack in the name of fairness. Oostburg might end up going the way of its neighbors. Preparing the way for this, socialists have been targeting civil society's essential partner, business.

CHAPTER 34

Woke Capitalism

Business used to stand up for traditional values. Look at corporate advertising from the 1950s, the golden age of civil society. The household and traditional gender roles are celebrated. And yet the advertisers knew whom to target. They understood that women were important economic actors, managing household finances, and so targeted them with ads for staples and labor-saving devices that would make their lives better. If the advertisers had been looking to promote a patriarchy, as critics of this age of advertising often suggest, they'd have targeted the husbands instead.

Businesses thereby performed three functions—they validated the existing institutions such as marriage and the household, promoted greater economic freedom and helped create wealth, and asserted their own importance as responsible pieces of the fabric of American society. In short, they understood American values.

But something changed. Many American businesses now use their marketing power not to stand up for American values, but to challenge them. Some companies' commercials and choices of spokespeople seem designed less to sell customers goods than to lecture them. Both internal and external corporate communications are permeated with political considerations. This is the phenomenon of "woke capitalism."

As my old boss Fred Smith used to say, businesses need to reach not only Joan Consumer, but also Joan Citizen. A company that advertises on nothing but price is only speaking to Joan Consumer. One that signals "we share your values" is speaking to Joan Citizen.

It's a technique as old as the hills. And yet modern corporations have discovered they can go further. They have at their fingertips vast networks they can use not just to appeal to Joan Citizen, but to influence her politically as well, thereby creating a feedback loop of political action in favor of both corporations' values. They have built up vast amounts of knowledge about consumers thanks to loyalty programs and tracking data from ads. They know whether their customers are politically active, and they know what issues motivate them.

As we know, young college-educated consumers are much more likely to be socialist than older Americans. They are likely to be unmarried, and to have high disposable income as a result of not being on the property ladder. They are also often transient, which means they don't have particular ties to a community.

If these are your networks, "woke capitalism" is a no-brainer. Mozilla's firing of Brendan Eich for giving money to a campaign against gay marriage was a legitimate business decision based on what the company knew about its consumers. Google's firing of James Damore was justified because of the need to quell the outrage among one of its most important networks—the engineers who build its products.

There is an obvious danger here. Woke capitalism may be at risk of intensifying a war between values groups. When Nike publicly backed Colin Kaepernick, they weren't just playing to their networks, they were telling their customers who value the American flag that they don't matter.

This is a far cry from how companies used to behave. They are setting themselves in opposition to civil society rather than being an important part of it—because of the influence of socialist thought.

It appears that the hope in some boardrooms is that if corporations are seen as being allies in the socialist transformation of America, they will not be nationalized or regulated to death. Moreover, socialist-inspired regulations can actually serve as entry barriers, giving a large corporation a virtual monopoly by stopping competitors from gaining size, or even from existing in the first place.

Because of the power of business networks, this attitude is a formidable problem. A woke bank may use a woke phone manufacturer and a woke telecom network to prevent us from spending our money at a disfavored establishment, such as a gun show. If the bank, phone manufacturer, and telecom network are the only game in town, we're sunk.

It should come as no surprise, therefore, that traditionalists (and some liberty-lovers) are calling for active government intervention to rein in the power of woke corporations.

PART FIVE

Socialism: A Temptation America Can't Afford to Indulge

CHAPTER 35

Tocqueville's Warning

A s we have seen, the French writer Alexis de Tocqueville was impressed by America's civic associations and how those strengthened its democracy. Yet Tocqueville was not Panglossian about America's constitutional design. He recognized that there were dangers in American democracy.

One of these was the scope for the tyranny of the majority. That was philosopher John Stuart Mill's description for the state of affairs when a majority of the people imposes harm on a minority. This might well be social as much as political—if a majority of people think, say, that Catholicism is a heresy, Catholics will end up being persecuted in some way. Democracy, however, exacerbates the chance of the tyranny of the majority's being imposed politically, and that's why we recognize rights.

Tocqueville laid out the dangers of what he called the "omnipotence of the majority": "When a man or a party suffers from an injustice in the United States, to whom do you want them to appeal? To public opinion? That is what forms the majority. To the legislative body? It represents the majority and blindly obeys it. To the executive power? It is named by the majority and serves it as a passive instrument. To the police? The police are nothing other than the majority under arms. To the jury? The jury is the majority vested with the right to deliver judgments. The judges themselves, in certain states, are elected by the majority."

Tocqueville contrasted America with states that had "mixed" constitutions and intermediary institutions, such as an aristocracy, that could prevent tyranny. He did recognize that both civic associations and the Bill of Rights acted as a brake on this power, but warned that even the courts interpreted those rights according to the opinions of the majority. Moreover, he noted, "I know of no country where, in general, there reigns less independence of mind and true freedom of discussion than in America."

While this may ring hollow to anyone engaged in political debate these days, there is considerable truth in what Tocqueville said. If a majority of the population does ever fall victim to the lure of socialism, it could become unstoppable.

We can see the long-term harm done by the Progressive Era and the New Deal, which represented a second and third American Revolution, imposed by the majorities of their day. Laws and institutions created then have achieved a quasi-constitutional status. It is very difficult to see a path to repeal of, for instance, the Fair Labor Standards Act (FLSA), whose definition of what an employment contract should look like continues to shape our working lives today, even as our needs have changed. Parents, for instance, want more flexibility in hours so they can be more involved in their children's lives than their great-grandparents were in the 1930s, yet the FLSA assumes employers want workers to work longer hours and grants overtime under certain circumstances while being silent on the flexibility of those hours.

Indeed, we can see the effect of the tyranny of the majority on "independence of mind" in action in, for example, our changing attitudes to comedy. Comedians used to poke fun at received wisdom and the attitudes of the establishment; today they reinforce them. Jerry Seinfeld, for instance, whose show "about nothing" poked fun at the lives of Manhattanites in the 1990s, notes that more and more comedians won't do shows on college campuses, for fear of offending the "politically correct" students.[1] As *The Coddling of the American Mind* tells us, those places where "independence of mind" used to be strengthened are now places where it is crushed.[2] Tocqueville was right.

Tocqueville therefore set out a plausible path by which socialism might establish itself in America. Imagine that socialism became the dominant ideology, and independent thought criticizing it was silenced. Elected officials and lawmakers instituted it. The courts, being affected by the lack of independence of mind (or by threats of court-packing), interpreted the Bill of Rights to allow socialism (free speech is interpreted as being about equality, for instance), and juries refuse to nullify the new laws. Opposition parties would have to accept the new socialist environment, being able to gain only modest repeals of the laws implementing it. After a generation or two, America would be a fully socialist state, awaiting the inevitable collapse that is the fate of all such regimes.

There are signs that this might already be happening. Another of Tocqueville's warnings tells us how democracy itself can be subverted: "After having…taken each individual one by one into its powerful hands, and having molded him as it pleases, the sovereign power extends its arms over the entire society; it covers the surface of society with a network of small, complicated, minute, and uniform rules, which the most original minds and the most vigorous souls cannot break through to go beyond the crowd; it does not break wills, but it softens them, bends them and directs them; it rarely forces action, but it constantly opposes your acting; it does not destroy, it

prevents birth; it does not tyrannize, it hinders, it represses, it ener-
vates, it extinguishes, it stupefies, and finally it reduces each nation
to being nothing more than a flock of timid and industrious animals,
of which the government is the shepherd."

Tocqueville called this "administrative despotism," and it would
likely be an easier path to socialism in America than "seizing control
of the commanding heights of the economy."

America is well on its way to becoming such an administrative
despotism. There are currently so many federal agencies that even
the federal government itself is unsure of how many there are.

Every year my colleague Wayne Crews compiles a report called
"Ten Thousand Commandments," mapping out the extent of the
administrative state.

These federal agencies issue rules that have the effect of law, as a
result of Congress's delegating them lawmaking power (something
that would appear to be unconstitutional on a plain reading of the
Constitution, although current legal doctrine says otherwise.) Wayne
points out that over the last decade agencies have on average issued
twenty-seven rules for every law passed by Congress.

Yet it's not just rules, which are subject to an official review process that allows for some formal involvement of affected parties. The
agencies also issue interpretations, rulings, circulars, guidance, and
other forms of "regulatory dark matter" that practically have the force
of law. The Obama administration issued one far-reaching decision
on employment law by blog post. Together these make up the "small,
complicated, minute, and uniform rules" that condition us to government interference in our lives.

This is the perfect vehicle for the creeping introduction of socialism. We don't talk about abolishing agencies any more. Instead, we
accept them and their rule-making powers. Every proposed deregulation is bitterly opposed as a weakening of "protection." We accept

that there will be a minimum wage, despite what it does to the lowest-skilled in our communities. The only thing we talk about is raising it by rule, not lowering it, and certainly not repealing it.

The machinery for a socialist takeover is already in place. Tocqueville warned us.

CHAPTER 36

You Can't Beat Government with Government

Why shouldn't we use government power to beat back woke capitalism? Why can't we use tariffs to stop jobs' going overseas? What possible justification is there for vulture capitalism destroying American communities? These are all questions American conservatives are asking right now.

The blunt answer is that the solutions usually suggested misdiagnose the problem. More important, they play into the hands of the socialists, making it much easier for them to implement socialism in America.

Take trade. We have already seen how the problem of forgotten America isn't so much a problem with trade as problems that the socialist policies we already have in place have caused in our culture, and problems with government rules stopping adaptation. Tariffs don't provide an answer to those problems. They only make them worse.

President Trump's trade war hurt Americans. It had to be mitigated by a vast new welfare program for American farmers. The $30 billion spent on making the effects of the trade war less severe was more than the Navy spends on new ships each year. It may prove to be temporary—if China keeps its promise to buy American agricultural produce at increased levels, but China has never been known for keeping its word in trade agreements.[1] Instead, we may have a new permanent welfare system, managed by bureaucrats, that could come under the control of a socialist administration.

Meanwhile, we have a trade system also managed by bureaucrats, with government officials responsible for deciding whether or not an import is exempt from tariffs. The public choice problem is obvious—research shows that exemptions are given to politically connected businesses, and not to those without crony connections.

Furthermore, the trade war has normalized the idea that tariffs can be used to promote domestic political interests. This had been the norm in the early twentieth century, but it contributed so much to global instability that America led the way in creating a new rules-based international order for trade, which reduced the problem considerably.

Socialists, however, are keen to use trade to tackle non-trade problems. We have already mentioned how the Green New Deal would impose carbon tariffs in an effort to reduce emissions. They will also restrict trade in order to impose environmental standards on developing nations, which will mean those nations will take much longer to develop, ensuring more people remain in poverty for longer. Similarly, they use trade to impose labor regulations on our trading partners. This strengthens the position of labor unions in the U.S. and again hurts people in developing countries by restricting their opportunities. And all these restrictions will raise the price we pay for goods in the United States, hurting our own standard of living. The normalization of trade wars will make these actions much more likely under a socialist administration.

What to do about "woke" and "vulture" capitalism is a thornier problem. These are private corporations, and as such under the traditional understanding of how American capitalism operates, they have every right to behave in the way they do.

The one exception to that traditional understanding is a period from the Progressive Era through the New Deal when government wielded antitrust power like a hammer, breaking up any company that got too big for its boots. It was a centerpiece of Theodore Roosevelt's, Woodrow Wilson's and FDR's administrations. In his 1944 State of the Union address, FDR proposed an economic "right of every businessman, large and small, to trade in an atmosphere of freedom from unfair competition and domination by monopolies at home or abroad." This was part of FDR's proposed "Second Bill of Rights" that he was unable to push through owing to his death, but which helped frame the positive rights orientation of many national constitutions after World War II. In many ways, it has dominated economic debate ever since.

American antitrust law, however, took a different turn, owing to the research and argument of conservative legal scholars like Judge Robert Bork. They found that the aggressive antitrust action of the first half of the twentieth century hurt American consumers. Large dominant companies like Standard Oil that were the target of antitrust action were delivering significant benefits to their customers, and had achieved their market power simply through being very good at their job. Breaking these companies up reduced the benefits to the consumer, stifled innovation, kept prices high, and benefitted inefficient competitors. Judges and regulators therefore instituted a "consumer welfare standard" that asked whether large companies were providing benefits to consumers; if so, the competition was not unfair.

Socialists have an ambivalent attitude to antitrust, echoing their love-hate relationship with the corporation. In a Marxist or democratic socialist state, nationalized industries will be monopolies. So monopolies could be seen as candidates for nationalization. In 1912, when he was running against the trustbuster Teddy Roosevelt, the socialist presidential candidate Eugene Debs said, "Monopoly is certain and sure. It is merely a question of whether they will be collectively owned monopolies, for the good of the race, or whether they will be privately owned for the power, pleasure and glory of the Morgans, Rockefellers, Guggenheims, and Carnegies."[2]

Senator Bernie Sanders, on the other hand, complains, "Without competition...corporations are able to gouge consumers, extort suppliers, and stifle innovation."[3] His solution is to take antitrust law out of the courts and put it in the hands of bureaucrats. Given that Senator Richard Sherman, who authored the first antitrust law in 1890, warned that the laws were necessary or else "the socialist, the communist, and the nihilist" would take over, you can see that there is no easy solution.

We need to apply Occam's Razor to the question of socialism and antitrust. The simple fact is that giving government power to intervene in markets means that it will be able to abuse that power. Socialists want to subjugate the individual to the collective, and antitrust power gives them ample opportunity to do so. Traditionalists should be very wary of normalizing bureaucratic intervention in our markets.

The answer to "woke capitalism" should never be to increase government power. At some point politicians and bureaucrats are going to start using their new powers against traditionalist interests. Instead, reforms should concentrate on the entry barriers that prevent competition—in other words, on opening up the possibility of the next Apple being founded in your neighbor's garage. That's an ideal as American as Apple pie.[4]

CHAPTER 37

America's Immunity to Socialism

W e should be grateful that socialism has not yet taken over the United States. America has proved resistant to the socialist temptation in a way no other country has. I have mentioned that I grew up in Britain, which brought its kings to heel in the name of liberty, which was the cradle of the Industrial Revolution, and which stood up to fascist tyranny when no one else would. It still became a socialist country in the 1940s. Over the past century, virtually every other country in the world has experimented with socialism in one form or another.

But America has resisted the charms of socialism. As we have seen, this has a lot to do with early American labor leaders like Samuel Gompers, who refused to back revolutionary politics. AFL-CIO leaders like George Meany and Lane Kirkland, who were strongly opposed to communism during the Cold War, built on the legacy of Gompers. While they may have had battles with capitalists at home, they were opposed to Marxism and nationalization—unlike their socialist brothers in Britain. Kirkland strongly supported Lech Walesa and the Solidarnosc trade union in Poland during their uprising against the communist authorities. As an aide to former Senator

Orrin Hatch told the *Washington Post* in 1983, "The AFL-CIO in general takes foreign policy positions to the right of Ronald Reagan."[1]

What changed was something that FDR, of all people, had warned about. In 1937 he said, "All Government employees should realize that the process of collective bargaining, as usually understood, cannot be transplanted into the public service. It has its distinct and insurmountable limitations when applied to public personnel management." In other words, he was opposed to collective bargaining between unions representing government employees and their bosses, who held their own employment in public trust. Even throughout the New Deal, government labor unions were without special privileges. That broke down when first the state of New York and then President John F. Kennedy granted them those privileges.

The result has been a massive swing in whom labor unions represent. Currently fewer than ten percent of American private sector workers belong to a labor union. But one in three government employees are union members. The actual numbers of union members are about equal—around 7 million in each sector. This has led to union bosses' rethinking what kind of America they want to see. Gompers, Meany, and Kirkland all represented a union workforce that had a vested interest in American free enterprise and sharing the fruits of capitalism. Current union leaders have much more invested in government, whose workforce and budget they want to grow.

This change was exemplified when Service Employees International Union (SEIU) president John Sweeney, who represented public sector workers alongside healthcare and property services workers, took control of the AFL-CIO in 1995 with the support of other government unions. Sweeney had joined the Democratic Socialists of America to show how much more radical he was than

Kirkland. Labor unions, once a bulwark against socialism, are now in its vanguard.

In the same way, American corporations once formed an impregnable bastion against socialism. American business leaders were happy to stand up for capitalism and were proud of their role in helping to build a prosperous American society. When business came under severe threat in the New Deal, businesses used their advertising networks to speak to Joan Citizen, underlining their support for American values.

And in 1934, John Jacob Raskob, a former General Motors executive, brought together businessmen and bipartisan politicians to create the American Liberty League, which pledged "to teach the necessity of respect for the rights of persons and property as fundamental to every successful form of government... teach the duty of government to encourage and protect individual and group initiative and enterprise, to foster the right to work, earn, save, and acquire property, and to preserve the ownership and lawful use of property when acquired." New Deal supporters accused the League of being "apostles of greed," and alleged that its aim was to "squeeze the worker dry in his old age and cast him like an orange rind into the refuse pail."

Despite its efforts, the American Liberty League backfired. Its reliance on a very few wealthy donors made it vulnerable to attack as a front for Dupont, while its bipartisanship enabled FDR to position himself as a truly independent voice. Roosevelt cruised to victory in 1936, and by 1940 the league had shut down all operations.

As my mentor Fred Smith said, "This failure persuaded many business leaders that resistance to the growth of government was futile and that they must accommodate themselves to an ever more politicized economy. Some noted that, after all, regulations and other interventions provided opportunities to gain some relative advantages, even at the expense of lost economic investment and operating freedom."[2]

As Smith noted, business leaders have proved accommodating to increased government interference in their activities since then. They have, moreover, tended to apologize for their activities rather than promoting them as fundamental to American values. The emergence of woke capitalism can be traced directly back to the failure of the American Liberty League.

With the retreat of business from the fray (with one exception that I'll come to later), resistance to socialism came mainly from a united conservative movement. With the emergence of the Soviet Union as a world power after WWII, socialism was linked more than ever to its extreme form, communism. The conservative movement consisted of three strands of thought, each vehemently opposed to communism. Defense hawks viewed communism as a military threat. Free marketeers stood against communism's economic system. Traditionalist conservatives were horrified by communism's militant atheism and rejection of Christian morality.

These strands of thought came together in what *National Review* editor Frank Meyer called fusionism. Meyer was convinced that libertarians and traditionalists needed each other. As he put it in his essay "Freedom, Tradition, Conservatism," the "belief in virtue as the end of men's being implicitly recognizes the necessity of freedom to choose that end; otherwise, virtue could be no more than a conditioned tropism.... truth withers when freedom dies, however righteous the authority that kills it; and free individualism uninformed by moral value rots at its core and soon brings about conditions that pave the way for surrender to tyranny."[3]

This synthesis of values served America well. New Deal progressivism never metastasized into socialism, which was left to European countries to experiment and fail with. Egalitarianism focused on race relations and civil liberties, where it succeeded in bringing injustices to light and righting past wrongs. Even the camel's nose in the tent of welfare was briefly pushed back out by a bipartisan alliance that achieved welfare reform in the 1990s.

This was the state of America when I arrived, suitcase in hand, in 1997. The idea that America might be susceptible to socialism was unthinkable then.

CHAPTER 38

Is It Different This Time?

America is different today. Americans are clearly tempted by socialism as they never have been before. But why is that? The fact is, we have allowed our institutions to be taken over by radicals. It's something the socialists have been planning for decades.

In the 1930s, Mussolini threw a communist by the name of Antonio Gramsci is prison. The ideas in the works that Gramsci wrote in prison have influenced subsequent generations of socialists. One of these was the idea that socialists needed to achieve "cultural hegemony," and that they could do so by waging a "war of position" that would facilitate revolution. Gramsci believed (rightly, as we have seen) that civil society could frustrate socialist revolutionary ambitions, so he advocated that socialists work to take over civil society and displace capitalism from its cultural hegemony.

Gramsci's tactics were eagerly adopted by the German socialist student movement of the 1960s. Student leader Rudi Dutschke advocated "der lange Marsch durch die Institutionen" to change institutions to remake civil society. In English, "the long march through the institutions" was praised by radical American leaders like our friend

Herbert Marcuse, who gave this definition: "working against the established institutions while working within them, but not simply by 'boring from within', rather by 'doing the job', learning (how to program and read computers, how to teach at all levels of education, how to use the mass media, how to organize production, how to recognize and eschew planned obsolescence, how to design, *et cetera*), and at the same time preserving one's own consciousness in working with others."[1]

This is precisely what has happened. Socialists have learned how to use our institutions—schools, colleges, and corporations—to advance their message. As we have seen, this is currently most pronounced in our institutions of higher learning and in large corporations. Grade-schoolers are taught that they can choose their own gender. Sports leagues have been cowed into the same apologetics as business was. Organized campaigns exist to drive people who say the unthinkable off social media platforms (often in collusion with platform executives), in other example of what Tocqueville was talking about when he worried about American independence of mind. *Wrongthink* is effectively outlawed.

Thoughtcrime is next. Even the concept that a man is free to vote according to his conscience has come under attack. Cultural critic Noah Berlatsky, the author of *Wonder Woman: Bondage and Feminism in the Marston/Peter Comics, 1941-1948*, has advanced the idea that casting a vote for racist reasons is unconstitutional, and that election law should be changed to reflect this.

At the same time, elected politicians have used their powers to hollow out civil society. The destruction of mutual societies was first. Welfarism and regulation have helped to snuff out self-help and enterprise in large parts of the country (and the socialists have placed the blame on free trade and capitalism), increasing alienation. Labor unions have become advocates for ever-increasing government power. Regulation is used to keep corporate executives that might stand up for free enterprise in their place. Religion is under attack as a central organizing force in society, except where it is organizing for socialist goals.

All of this is facilitated by that second constitution we discussed back in Chapter 1—the parallel constitution of super-statutes—and what has been called "administrative constitutionalism," the idea that bureaucrats have a constitutional status.

Our institutions of liberty have either been captured, weakened, or are next on the list. So far, the military appears to have been somewhat immune to capture, but with the Pentagon treating climate change as a national security threat and the Army Corps of Engineers having been designated a central role in interfering with private citizens' property rights through environmental law, it is clear that it is under target.

The 2016 presidential election was a major shock to the long marchers. They had believed that a Hillary Clinton presidency would allow them to capture more of the institutions, including the Supreme Court and the entire judiciary.

CHAPTER 39

Conservative Infighting

O ne factor that has helped strengthen the hand of the long marchers is conservative infighting. As we have seen, conservative unity played a major role in suppressing socialism over the past half century.

But those days are gone. Fusionism has broken down, perhaps irrevocably. Defense hawks are now viewed with suspicion by libertarians and traditionalists alike. Libertarians hate the way they advocate for bloated defense budgets and drag America into needless wars. Traditionalists often also hate the wars, which they feel are needlessly killing good young men and destroying families in the process.

Libertarians, meanwhile, are viewed as peaceniks by the defense hawks, but are the particular target of ire from traditionalists. Traditionalists allege that libertarians have sold out American communities in pursuit of the almighty Dollar and have enthusiastically supported the creation of telecommunications and entertainment infrastructures that are destroying American culture. Traditionalists increasingly want libertarians drummed out of the conservative movement in the way William F. Buckley dealt with the John Birch Society.

Many libertarians, on the other hand, just cannot understand traditionalists. Libertarians view traditionalists as undermining the success of the American economy with their support for trade wars, and overall failing to understand basic economics. Defense hawks, who want allies who will support their policies on the Middle East, are frustrated by traditionalists' increasing isolationism.

The infighting is intensified by another divide—between populists and establishment conservatives. Establishment conservatives view some tactics that populists revel in as beyond the pale. Populists ask what exactly have establishment conservatives managed to conserve and view them as worse than useless, while establishment conservatives worry about mass rallies, intemperate language, and the temptation not of socialism but of fascism.

Attitudes to the polarizing figure of President Trump loom large in all of this. Is he the savior of the conservative movement, or the sign of its implosion? Libertarians praise his deregulation while condemning his trade policy. Traditionalists love his defense of American communities and religion but worry about the example his personal behavior has set. Defense hawks love his firm actions against Iran but worry about his withdrawal from Syria. On virtually every area of administration policy there is heated internal debate within the movement.

This gives opportunities to the socialists. The old Roman maxim of *divide et impera* (divide and conquer) holds true for them. Disputes over trade policy allow them to side with traditionalists while at the same time planning for carbon tariffs and using trade policy to enhance labor rules in their favor. Disquiet with foreign policy is an opportunity for a reduction in military spending and the weakening of the military as a cultural institution.

Above all, the discrediting of capitalism is a heaven-sent circumstance that allows the socialists to present socialism as the only reasonable alternative. It is an old Marxist trick to make socialism seem reasonable by "heightening the contradictions" of capitalist society. If capitalism builds wealth, why are there so many poor people? If free enterprise doesn't hurt the environment, why is global warming accelerating? If credit enables opportunity, why are so many people crippled by debt? When conservatives ask the same questions rather than remembering that no system is perfect, socialists smile.

Nevertheless, the cracks in conservatism have tended to be papered over when elections are on the line. Whether that will be true in 2020 remains to be seen.

CHAPTER 40

Reagan's Challenge

We have reached the point that President Reagan warned about in his speech at Hillsdale College in 1977: "It all comes down to this basic premise: if you lose your economic freedom, you lose your political freedom, and in fact all freedom. Freedom is something that cannot be passed on genetically. It is never more than one generation away from extinction. Every generation has to learn how to protect and defend it. Once freedom is gone, it's gone for a long, long time. Already, too many of us, particularly those in business and industry, have chosen to switch rather than fight."

If we are to pass freedom on to our children we have to rise to the occasion as Reagan and the Reaganauts did in the 1970s and 1980s. President Reagan recognized that this was, above all, a communications challenge. He said, "Why don't more of us challenge what Cicero called the arrogance of officialdom? Why don't we set up communications between organizations and trade associations? To rally others to come to the aid of an individual like that, or to an industry or profession when they're threatened by the barons of bureaucracy, who have forgotten that we are their employers.

Government by the people works when the people work at it. We can begin by turning the spotlight of truth on the widespread political and economic mythology that I mentioned...."

To win this battle against Big Government, we must communicate with each other. We must support the doctor in his fight against socialized medicine, the oil industry in its fight against crippling controls and repressive taxes, and the farmer, who hurts more than most because of government harassment and rule-changing in the middle of the game. All of these issues concern each one of us, regardless of what our trade or profession may be.

This challenge is made all the harder by some of the problems we have looked at in the last few chapters. Officialdom has more powers at its disposal today; court challenges take time and resources most people don't have. Professions and corporations have been suborned. One poll found that 49 percent of physicians support Medicare for All; the oil industry supports carbon taxes; farmers are the recipients of billions of dollars of agri-welfare.[1]

That means that communication between groups is more difficult; it does not make it impossible. We still have the advantage of the spotlight of truth. History is on our side.

Moreover, this isn't the first time we have been in this situation. The last time around, the American Liberty League was one failed response. Another, which might have helped inspire President Reagan's thinking, came in 1971.

CHAPTER 41

The Powell Memorandum

In 1971, a lawyer from Richmond, Virginia, named Lewis F. Powell Jr. wrote a memorandum for a businessman who shared it with the U.S. Chamber of Commerce. It was entitled "Attack on the American Free Enterprise System." Powell, who two months after the memo was written would be nominated to the Supreme Court, had been inspired to write the memo by a series of attacks on capitalism by the likes of Herbert Marcuse and the activist Ralph Nader, whom he decried as "openly seek[ing] destruction of the system."

Powell began, "There always have been some who opposed the American system, and preferred socialism or some form of statism (communism or fascism).... But what now concerns us is quite new in the history of America. We are not dealing with sporadic or isolated attacks from a relatively few extremists or even from the minority socialist cadre. Rather, the assault on the enterprise system is broadly based and consistently pursued. It is gaining momentum and converts."

Lewis Powell was a strategist of the highest order. A distinguished educator as well as a lawyer, he had clearly thought through the problem deeply. He recommended a program of counter-attack and communications that included several ideas that might have seemed "out of the box" in the 1970s. They included:

- Focus on the American campus as the hotbed of radicalism (this sounds horribly familiar, does it not?), with a board of distinguished scholars who "do believe in the system," a speaker's program, evaluation of textbooks, insistence on equal time for speakers, a long-term program aimed at balance in faculty, and particular engagement with business schools

- Communicate with the public through monitoring television news broadcasts, publishing commentary in popular and "highbrow" news outlets, publishing books, paperbacks, and pamphlets, and devoting 10 percent of business advertising budgets to defending free enterprise

- Engage directly with politicians. Powell noted that "political power is necessary; that such power must be assid[u]ously cultivated; and that when necessary, it must be used aggressively and with determination—without embarrassment and without the reluctance which has been so characteristic of American business"

- Create a litigation program aimed at defending American business in the courts, using the amicus process (legal arguments about the case submitted by outside parties as "friends of the court"). As Powell pointed out, "with an activist-minded Supreme Court, the judiciary may be the most important instrument for social, economic and political change"

- Motivate America's 20 million stockholders to engage in the educational and political process

Powell noted that such a program would be very costly, and would require significant quality control. This would be justified, however, for a very simple reason: "The threat to the enterprise system is not merely a matter of economics. It also is a threat to individual freedom... There seems to be little awareness that the only alternatives to free enterprise are varying degrees of bureaucratic regulation of individual freedom—ranging from that under moderate socialism to the iron heel of the leftist or rightist dictatorship."[1]

Powell's advice was heeded, after a fashion. Businessmen helped set up think tanks, most notedly the Heritage Foundation, to provide heavyweight intellectual firepower. Student groups were supported, and speakers provided. After a regulatory change, talk radio and cable news channels were founded. Books, articles, and op-eds were printed. Politicians were persuaded to found groups like the Republican Study Committee and the House Freedom Caucus (the Gingrich revolution was probably the apogee of this effort.) Amicus briefs were filed, court cases were brought, and groups like the Federalist Society enabled conservative lawyers and judges to sharpen conservative thought on legal issues.[2]

Powell's strategy was so successful that socialist and environmentalist groups condemn it to this day. Greenpeace, for instance, calls his memo "a blueprint for corporate domination of American Democracy."[3] Whole books have been written about how business "stole the American dream."

Yet, thirty years later, the wheel has come full circle. Everything that Powell complained about has reasserted itself, despite the strategy he outlined. Once again we face a challenge of communication.

CHAPTER 42

Meeting Reagan's Challenge

A
s I have tried to suggest in this book, the resurgence of socialism owes much to the way it speaks to fundamental American values. Any modern response to the socialist temptation must attempt to do the same, or it will surely fail.

This may have been the problem with the Powell approach, successful as it was for a while. Powell's academic approach and his concentration on analysis produced plenty of good arguments and good ideas, but all at the level of what Hayek called the "war of ideas." Hayek believed that, as policy was generally set by an educated intellectual class, all that was needed was to win the war of ideas at that level and all would be well.

But the resurgence of socialism shows that that's not enough. Ideas surge up as well as trickle down. Furthermore, the popularity of socialist ideas among the most educated class suggests that even the argument at the intellectual level is being lost.

A lot of it has to do with how people who support the free market system speak. My friend Professor Steve Horwitz of Ball State University believes that economists and free-marketers bear some responsibility for the resurgence of socialism because of the way they frame their arguments: "How often do we speak of markets as sources of not just prosperity, but prosperity for the least well off? How often do we speak of markets as the cause of peace and social cooperation and mutual interdependence? How often do we talk about how markets have humanized us and reduced our propensity to violence, and turned strangers into honorary friends or kin? It's important to stress the material wealth that markets produce, but the point of even that is enabling us to live lives of peace, cooperation, and security."[1]

Horwitz talks about the "double thank you" of the marketplace—where each participant in an economic transaction thanks the other—as emblematic of how markets and economic exchanges bring us together. Yet too often we allow people to think of economic transactions as exploitative.

Moreover, along the way, free marketers forgot how to talk to their closest allies, traditionalists. Some libertarians have grown disdainful of traditionalist concerns about community and alienation, dismissing them as "victimhood." They have forgotten, or failed to make the argument, that freedom and tradition go hand in hand in America, and one without the other weakens them both, opening the door for the authoritarian solutions of socialism.

If we are to meet Reagan's challenge, then, we need to learn how to speak the language of values when defending American capitalism. This is particularly important in the age of social media. People tend to share articles and stories that support their worldview, their fundamental values.

Moreover, as Horwitz implies, stories are all-important. Free marketers have concentrated too much on economic analysis and aggregating things to the national level, which provides mind-blowingly huge numbers, but is hard to relate to the household level. Every argument should include some talk about what it means for the average household, told at a relatable level.

Stories are even better when they include some testimony. An old colleague of mine used to talk about how a good communicator had a Ph.D.—the ability to Personalize, Humanize, and Dramatize an issue. This was something President Reagan was very good at. Just before he called for better communications, he told this story:

> Up in Pocatello, Idaho, was a man, elderly man, with grown sons. They owned a sub-contracting plumbing and electrical firm—thirty-five employees. He had known that someday they would get to his door, and he'd wondered what he would do. And he knew about—he'd heard about the woman in New Mexico. Sure enough, they came to his door, and he said, "not without a warrant." And they read him paragraph 8(a) of the OSHA Act. And he pointed to a framed copy of the Constitution on the wall of his office and said, "I think there's a higher law." Well they came back not with a warrant, but with a court order. He defied it. He was cited for contempt. He got a lawyer. Now his friends, and even the lawyer tried to talk him out of it. They said, "You can't fight the government. That's too big for you." And just love what he said to his friends. He said, "You know, we send our young fellas out to fight and die for freedom. Maybe it's time some of us old duffers did something for a change."[2]

It's a great story, not just because it tells the tale of how one man can fight back against bureaucracy, but because it contains a call to action—the idea that we all should be doing "something for a change."

This brings me to a second recommendation. Part of the story of this book is how we have allowed bulwarks against socialism to be torn down—or to wear away—over the years. In biology, there is the concept of the "inhibitor," something that blocks the progress of a disease. These bulwarks were the inhibitors that protected our system against socialism. We need to build them back.

One inhibitor was our associations, particularly mutual societies. Laws and regulations over the years have given privileges to other forms of corporate organization, such as health insurance companies, that have crowded out mutual societies. We need a thorough review of those laws and regulations and a program of repeal that will allow the space for associations to start up again, and we need some brave people to take the lead and help to form these associations.

One form of association that is still going strong but has lost its way is the labor union. American labor unions, as we've seen, used to exist symbiotically with capitalist corporations. Removing some of the privileges that make them more political would be a start. For example, making unions responsible only for their own members' bargaining and ending forced dues collection from non-members would make them more responsive to their members' interests. This could well make them less interested in lobbying government for more powers and more interested in things like offering a low-interest branded credit card.

Finally, the conservative movement needs to stop its infighting. Better internal communication like I outlined above will help, but at the very least conservatives need to realize that the socialist threat is very real and unite against it. A unified conservative movement is the best inhibitor we have seen against socialism. We must not allow the socialists' "heightening of the contradictions" to divide us.

CHAPTER 43

Heightening the Contradictions

We should be turning the tables on the socialists—heightening the contradictions in socialism. As we have seen:

- Socialism claims to be democratic, but necessarily leads to rule by bureaucrats
- As George Orwell said, socialism is a system where "all animals are equal but some are more equal than others."
- Socialism requires *doublethink*—particularly that a bigger, more powerful state will lead to the "withering away" of the state
- Freedom is maintained by coercion in the socialist state
- To a socialist, freedom of speech should not be allowed if it contributes to inequality
- Any revealed preference of the working class against socialist ideals is explained away as the product of false consciousness
- Socialism preserves community by tearing down its most sacred values

- The most important socialist virtue is brotherly love, which is achieved by making people dependent on state welfare
- And, above all, any attempt to create a socialist state is inevitably decried as "not real socialism"

We must not be shy about pointing out these contradictions.

Furthermore, we should be relentless in pinning them down on the question of what sort of socialism they want.

If they claim all they want is to be like Sweden, will they accept things like more capitalism and school choice in exchange for higher taxes and a bigger welfare state?

If they claim they want Marxism, but with democratic control of officials, ask them exactly how that will work.

If they want centrally planned economies, ask them how they solve the knowledge problem Mises identified.

If they want nationalized industries, ask them how they will overcome public choice problems.

If they express concern for the poor, ask how is it that it has been freer markets that have lifted billions out of poverty, while socialist regimes like the one in Venezuela inevitably reduce their citizens to starvation.

Above all, ask them how they plan to avoid the mistakes of past socialist experiments, and have Kristian Niemietz's rejoinder ready: "When critics of socialism bring up the oppressive nature of past socialist regimes, the intention is not to score rhetorical points against their opponents. The intention is to draw attention to the fact that these systems were not just randomly oppressive. They were all oppressive in similar ways. There are recognizable, recurring patterns of oppression under socialist regimes, and they are intimately linked with socialist economics."[1]

When you find them retreating to social democracy, then the battle is almost won. You can point out that most social democracies regard themselves as capitalist states—Sweden has a high percentage of billionaires—and say that socialism clearly isn't the solution they're looking for. Then the debate is about the size and effectiveness of the welfare state, and that's a completely different argument from the one about capitalism and socialism.

CHAPTER 44

Corbynism Routed

An example of how to fight back against socialism effectively
came while I was writing this book. As I mentioned earlier,
"magic grandad" Jeremy Corbyn had seized control of the
British Labour party and made it an explicitly radical socialist party
once again.

American democratic socialists praised this development. In *The
Socialist Manifesto*, Bhaskar Sunkara wrote, "Corbyn's breakthrough
has shown that socialists can garner popular support by building a
credible opposition rooted in an unapologetically left vision—that
is, by offering hopes and dreams, not just fear and diminished expec-
tations.... Class-struggle social democracy has the potential to win
a major national election today."

Corbyn's chance came in December 2019. Facing a Conservative
Party that had been ripped apart by divisions over the European
Union—to the extent that the second most powerful man in the previous prime minister's government, former Chancellor Philip Ham-
mond, found himself expelled from the party—Corbyn stood a good
chance of winning. Not only did he have his own Momentum movement of left-wing activists, he also had the support of the pro–EU

229

Remain movement, which had regularly flooded the streets of London with many thousands of activists opposed to Boris Johnson's signature policy of leaving the EU. This activist base, made up mostly of energetic, enthusiastic, and ideologically committed young people, would surely propel him to victory.

He lost. Decisively, ignominiously. It was the worst showing by a Labour leader in living memory, worse even than Soviet-appeasing Michael Foot in the mid-1980s.

Not only did he lose, he lost districts it was inconceivable for any Labour leader to ever lose. Tony Blair's old constituency of Sedgefield in County Durham for instance (the county where I grew up) and some surrounding districts had never voted conservative, at least since the Great Reform Act in the 1830s. It went Conservative by a comfortable margin. Labour won only one seat from the Conservatives, a central London seat (the hotbed of Remain activism), and its vote share collapsed around the country.

Corbyn's supporters claimed they had won the argument and that if it weren't for Brexit their popular policies would have propelled them to victory. As I write, the newly elected Labour leader, Sir Keir Starmer, has kept on most of Corbyn's socialist colleagues in his shadow cabinet. The socialist policies will continue.

But Boris Johnson campaigned on the three values we've discussed in this book—investing in social services and delivering a fairer tax system for a fairer society, supporting freedom by making Britain "the best place in the world" to start a business and freeing the United Kingdom from EU regulation, and addressing community and tradition by reviving Britain's towns and strengthening Britain in the world. It was an unabashedly optimistic message.

By contrast, Corbyn looked as if he was stuck in the 1970s. As *Foreign Policy* writer Andrew Brown put it, voters "will always reject politicians who claim that no one will have to pay for anything...."

The people, it turned out, did not concede to socialism the moral authority that socialists thought self-evident. Capitalism seemed more likely to deliver what it promised."

Boris Johnson took socialism to the woodshed by appealing to the wide range of British values. Beating socialism in American will require a similar approach—a strong defense of American values is the only way to resist the socialist temptation.

Socialism in the Age of Coronavirus

A fter this book was written, the world was stricken with the coronavirus, or Wuhan Flu, pandemic. Governments all over the world, and especially in the West, moved to enact wave after wave of what I term "flash policy" aimed variously at restricting the transmission of the disease, easing strain on the healthcare industry, preserving jobs during lockdown, and compensating the unemployed. The long-term effect of these waves of flash policy are yet to be seen, but they have been in place long enough to give us some clues about what they mean for the advance of socialism that we have been discussing.

Historians have often noted that pandemics and emergencies tend to reinforce and hasten trends and tendencies that were in place before the calamity occurred. In this case, we should not be surprised if the drift towards socialism among the young and educated intensifies. There are indications that this is precisely what is happening.

In particular, the different value groups I described in the book have reacted differently to both the virus and the lockdowns. Egalitarians saw a threat to the vulnerable and wanted to eliminate the virus risk entirely. Libertarians saw a threat to freedom from lockdowns and wanted that threat lifted as soon as possible. Traditionalists saw a particular threat to their religious lives from overly restrictive lockdowns, while some saw just as much of a threat from the virus itself.

Socialists were quick to see a policy opportunity. One of the waves of flash policy I mentioned was for "unemployment insurance on steroids." The CARES Act included a provision that anyone who was unemployed as a result of the virus would get an extra $600 a week on top of his normal unemployment benefit. This was nothing less than a stealth increase in the minimum wage. Who would go back to work unless they got the equivalent of their new combined benefits? Many employers who laid off their staff realized this immediately.

Another of the flash policies was a cash handout of $1200 per person with an additional $500 per child. Socialists were quick to say that the one-off payment was not enough and that it would need to be repeated. At time of writing, it has not happened, but with over 40 million people out of work, there is likely to be repeated clamor for additional payments. This is essentially the introduction of a Universal Basic Income as discussed earlier in the book—without the elimination of welfare-dependency benefit programs that could possibly make it acceptable.

Meanwhile, the healthcare sector is on the verge of collapse. Doctor's offices have closed as people are scared to see their physicians. Hospitals have canceled elective procedures to make room for virus patients, and then found they had empty beds and no income. The chances of single-payer healthcare being instituted as a rescue mechanism have skyrocketed.

If these three policies outlive the virus then America will in essence have been turned into a Scandinavian-style social democracy—but one with much more regulation of private industry. Bureaucracy and dependency will be the winners despite government bureaucracy at the CDC and FDA having hindered America's initial response to the crisis.

If, however, we are to keep the cash payments and unemployment benefits rolling and bail out the healthcare sector with a radical restructuring towards single-payer, then that will have to be paid for somehow. Either we all become Modern Monetary Theorists and just 'borrow from ourselves' or we will have to live with significantly increased taxes, or possibly both. Expropriation in the name of the common good will be back.

In other words, socialists are likely to come out of the virus strengthened, even as the economy reels.

There is, however, one silver lining. The crisis exposed that bureaucracy is a big problem. Not only did the public health agencies spend all their time worrying about vaping and global warming instead of infectious diseases, but when the disease came along, they messed up the initial tests, allowing the virus to take hold.

Furthermore, governors around the country trying to mitigate the economic damage of their lockdowns realized that they each were responsible for hundreds of regulations that stood in the way. Bans on delivering alcohol or on telemedicine provision were hastily lifted. Even Massachusetts and San Francisco which had previously encouraged reusable grocery bags, banned them because of their known ability to spread pathogens.

It has become apparent to everyone that many regulations were simply never needed in the first place. President Trump recognized this in late May by issuing an executive order instructing agencies to make permanent any temporary suspensions of regulations and telling them to eliminate more rules that could impede recovery. Socialists will oppose this, arguing that they need more regulation and more bureaucrats to secure a safe world for everyone. This is likely where the battle for the future of the American economy will take place. The bureaucratic paradise of the Green New Deal will be pitched against deregulation and a free economy.

If the socialists win, we face the prospect of a repeat of the Great Depression and New Deal-like policies that helped prolong it. A plethora of bureaucrats will attempt to run our lives for our own good and will do so at our expense. We will be running down Friedrich Hayek's road to serfdom.

When our health is at stake, we will listen to anyone who offers the hope of a cure. In the case of this virus, it may be that the worst snake oil is ideological—the socialist temptation.

Acknowledgements

I 'd like to thank all those who helped make this book possible. Thanks are due first to my wife, Kristen, for putting up with my being at home much more often than usual (which, in retrospect, helped us prepare for the lockdowns.) Secondly, thanks to my boss Kent Lassman, for allowing me the latitude to see the project through. My colleagues Wayne Crews, Sam Kazman, Travis Burk, John Berlau, Ryan Young, and Richard Morrison were excellent sounding-boards and helped me avoid going down blind alleys. I'd also like to thank the economists Steve Horwitz and Steve Davies, who each inspired at least part of this book and whose Facebook discussions provided yet more inspiration. The team at Regnery— Harry Crocker, my truly excellent editor Elizabeth Kantor, and Laura Swain—have all worked tirelessly to turn my inchoate thoughts into a cohesive reality. Finally, I could not have even thought of writing this book without learning at the feet of my mentor Fred Smith, to whom this book is dedicated.

Notes

Chapter 1: A Twenty-First-Century Buzzword

1. Meet the Press, "Ocasio-Cortez: Socialism Is 'Part of What I Am, Not All of What I Am,'" NBC News, July 1, 2018, https://www.nbcnews.com/meet-the-press/video/ocasio-cortez-socialism-is-part-of-what-i-am-not-all-of-what-i-am-1267955267646.

Chapter 2: What Is This Socialism Thing, Anyway?

1. Kristian Niemitz, *Socialism: The Failed Idea that Never Dies*, (London: London Publishing Partnership, 2019), 18.
2. David Henderson, The Concise Encyclopedia of Economics (Carmel, Indiana: Liberty Fund, 2007), "Fascism."
3. Von Mises, Ludwig. *Human Action: A Treatise on Economics*, (Chicago: Henry Regnery Company, 1966), Chapter 27, Section 2.
4. It is comforting to think that your employer's tax contribution comes from the employer's profits and not from your paycheck, but it isn't true. The money the employer sends to the state is money they could, and almost certainly would, pay you instead. Fredrik Carlgren, "Marginal Tax in Sweden and Internationally," Ekonomifakta.se, December 20, 2019, https://www.ekonomifakta.se/Fakta/Skatter/Skatt-pa-arbete/Marginalskatt/.

Chapter 3: Socialism in American History

1. David Cannadine, *Mellon: An American Life* (New York: A. A. Knopf, 2006), 444–45.
2. The *Lochner* case itself involved a racist labor union for bakery workers attempting to use the political process to limit competition

from immigrant Italian and Jewish bakers who were willing to work longer hours.

3. Once again, this may not have been a fight for equality. It seems that various attempts to impose minimum wages for women were an attempt to stop women coming into the workforce.
4. *Gonzales v. Raich*, 545 U.S. 1 (2005).
5. John T. Flynn, *The Roosevelt Myth* (Auburn, Alabama: Ludwig von Mises Institute, 2008).
6. Commissioner Humphrey died before his case could be heard, so it passed to his estate, hence *Humprey's Executor*.
7. For a great example, watch the 1933 Jimmy Durante propaganda film for the NRA called "Give a Man a Job" on your favorite video service. It ends with Durante pointing to a picture of FDR, flanked by eagles, and singing, "If the old name of Roosevelt / Makes your old heart throb / Then take this message, straight from the President / And give a man a job!" Both the message and the presentation are straight out of Mussolini's playbook.

Chapter 4: What Do the Polls Tell Us?
1. Robby Soave, "Socialism Is Back, and the Kids Are Loving It," *Reason*, August/September 2019, https://reason.com/2019/07/06/socialism-is-back-and-the-kids-are-loving-it/.
2. Emily Ekins, "What Americans Think about Poverty, Wealth, and Work: Findings from the Cato Institute 2019 Welfare, Wealth, and Work National Survey," Cato Institute, 2019, https://www.cato.org/sites/cato.org/files/2019-09/Cato2019WelfareWorkWealthSurveyReport%20%281%29.pdf.
3. Frank Newport, "Democrats More Positive about Socialism Than Capitalism, Gallup, August 13, 2018, https://news.gallup.com/poll/240725/democrats-positive-socialism-capitalism.aspx.

4. Felix Salmon, "Gen Z Prefers 'Socialism' to 'Capitalism,'" Axios, January 27, 2019, https://www.axios.com/socialism-capitalism-poll-generation-z-preference-1ffb8800-0ce5-4368-8a6f-de3b82662347.html.

5. Lydia Saad, Jeffrey M. Jones, and Megan Brenan, "Understanding Shifts in Democratic Party Ideology," Gallup, February 19, 2019, https://news.gallup.com/poll/246806/understanding-shifts-democratic-party-ideology.aspx.

6. "Fall 2018 National Youth Poll," Harvard Kennedy School Institute of Politics, 2018, https://iop.harvard.edu/spring-2018-national-youth-poll.

7. My native Britain has single-payer and state-provider healthcare, probably the worst of both worlds. Britons tend to believe that the National Health Service is the "envy of the world"—which is rather odd, considering that virtually no other country has copied the model.

8. The Paris Commune of 1870 had something like a jobs guarantee. They had gangs of people digging holes, and then other gangs filling them in.

9. "Labor > Trade Union Membership: Countries Compared," Nation Master, n.d., https://www.nationmaster.com/country-info/stats/Labor/Trade-union-membership.

10. Frank Newport, "The Meaning of 'Socialism' to Americans Today," Gallup, October 14, 2018, https://news.gallup.com/opinion/polling-matters/243362/meaning-socialism-americans-today.aspx.

Chapter 5: Socialism on Campus

1. Phil Magness, "Here Is Proof That the Leftist Tilt on Campus Has Gotten Dramatically Worse," AIER, May 1, 2019, https://www.aier.org/article/here-is-proof-that-the-leftist-tilt-on-campus-has-gotten-dramatically-worse/.

2. Helen Pluckrose, James A. Lindsay, and Peter Boghossian, "Academic Grievance Studies and the Corruption of Scholarship, Areo, October 2, 2018, https://areomagazine.com/2018/10/02/academic-grievance-studies-and-the-corruption-of-scholarship/.

3. Phillip Magness, "Commie Chic & Quantifying Marx on the Syllabus," Philmagness, August 15, 2016, http://philmagness.com/?p=1804.

4. Open Syllabus figures as of March 28, 2020, https://opensyllabus.org/results-list/titles?size=50; Plato's *Republic* is often thought of as a proto-socialist text, as it describes an "ideal" government that includes various forms of communal property. At heart, however, Plato's constitution is a metaphor for the soul and should not be taken too literally.

5. "8 in 10 Philosophy Majors Favor Socialism," College Pulse, July 11, 2019, https://collegepulse.com/2019/07/8-in-10-philosophy-majors-favor-socialism.html.

6. Phillip Magness, "How a Leftist Echo Chamber Became the New Norm on Campus," American Institute for Economic Research, July 17, 2019, https://www.aier.org/article/how-a-leftist-echo-chamber-became-the-new-norm-on-campus/.

7. Michael C. Munger, "On the Origins and Goals of Public Choice," *Independent Institute*, June 29, 2017, http://www.independent.org/issues/article.asp?id=9115.

8. Marc Parry, "Nancy MacLean Responds to Her Critics, *Chronicle of Higher Education*, July 19, 2017, https://www.chronicle.com/article/Nancy-MacLean-Responds-to-Her/240699/.

9. Ibid.

10. Greg Lukianoff and Jonathan Haidt, "The Coddling of the American Mind," *The Atlantic*, September 2015, https://www.theatlantic.com/magazine/archive/2015/09/the-coddling-of-the-american-mind/399356/.

Chapter 6: Cultural Cognition and American Values

1. The best approachable introduction to Wildavskian theory is Brendon Swedlow, "Aaron Wildavsky's Cultural Values Theory," in the "Competitive Enterprise Institute and National Media, Inc., Field Guide for Effective Communications," Competitive Enterprise Institute, 2004.

2. Despite their claims to respect science, Extinction Rebellion climate activists make claims that are in no way supported by mainstream climate science. "Billions will die" and "Your children will starve in twenty years" are much more an example of science denial than the skepticism of people like me, who acknowledge that the world is warming but point out that the proposed solutions will be harmful.

3. Arnold Kling, *The Three Languages of Politics: Talking Across the Political Divides* (Washington D.C.: Cato Institute, 2017).

4. Note that this argument is different from the argument of libertarians like Charles Murray, who contends that in a world where the argument over welfare has been lost, a UBI would be a better method of distribution than one where bureaucrats pick winners and losers.

5. You may remember the Redskins. They were a great American football team in the 1980s and 1990s. I am not sure what happened to them.

Chapter 7: The Socialist Position

1. "Toby Young Destroys Socialism in One Sentence," Politics Live, June 14, 2019, https://order-order.com/2019/06/14/toby-young-destroys-socialism-one-sentence/.

Chapter 8: The Gentleman in Washington, D.C., Knows Best

1. Richard Toye, "'The Gentleman in Whitehall' Reconsidered: The Evolution of Douglas Jay's Views on Economic Planning and Consumer Choice, 1937–47," *Labour History Review* (2003): 67.
2. In Friedrich A. Hayek, ed., *Collectivist Economic Planning* (Clifton, New Jersey: Kelley Publishing, 1975), 87–130.
3. Friedrich A. Hayek, "The Use of Knowledge in Society," *American Economic Review* 35, no. 4 (1945): 519–30.
4. "What Is Democratic Socialism," Democratic Socialists of America, https://www.dsausa.org/about-us/what-is-democratic-socialism/#govt.
5. This is in essence, the economic maxim known as Say's Law, often roughly summed up as "supply creates its own demand."

Chapter 9: Democratic Socialism in Action

1. This long predated socialist government—an 1880 court ruling held that the telephone was actually a telegram system, and the Post Office held a monopoly on telegrams. International cables, however, were owned by a private company called Cable & Wireless, which was nationalized and integrated into the Post Office system in 1947.

Chapter 10: The Socialist Death Toll

1. Malcolm Muggeridge (anonymously), "The Soviet and the Peasantry, An Observer's Notes," *Manchester Guardian*, March 27,1933.
2. Ibid.
3. Roderick MacFarquhar and Michael Schoenhals, *Mao's Last Revolution* (Cambridge, Massachusetts: Harvard University Press, 2006.)

4. Kenneth M. Quinn, former U.S. Ambassador to Cambodia, quoted in Hinton, Alexander and Lifton, Robert Jay, *Why Did They Kill?: Cambodia in the Shadow of Genocide* (Oakland, California: University of California Press, 2004).

5. Guerra, Weildler, "La dieta de Maduro," *El Espectador*, July 8, 2016.

6. Ciara Nugent, "How Hunger Fuels Crime and Violence in Venezuela," *Time*, October 23 2018.

7. Jonathan Chait, "100 Years after the Bolshevik Revolution, Communism Hasn't Changed," *New York Magazine*, June 28, 2017.

Chapter 11: Socialized Medicine and the NHS

1. Because fewer Brits own a TV set these days, there is pressure to extend this license fee to everyone in order to ensure the BBC's continued existence.

2. "Universal Healthcare without the NHS," Institute of Economic Affairs, December 2016, https://iea.org.uk/publications/universal-healthcare-without-the-nhs/.

Chapter 12: The Bureaucrat

1. Arthur Seldon, *The Virtues of Capitalism (The Collected Works of Arthur Seldon)* (Indianapolis, Indiana: Liberty Fund, 2004).

2. Bhaskar Sunkara notes that the founder of the KGB, Felix Dzerzhinsky, "anguished over every execution order he signed. He was replaced by men with no such compunction." (*The Socialist Manifesto*, 103). I am sure that Dzerzhinsky's tears were of great comfort to the families of his victims. Bhaskar Sunkara, *The Socialist Manifesto: The Case for Radical Politics in an Era of Extreme Inequality* (New York: Hachette, 2019).

3. "Interview: Introduction to India's Experience with Central Planning," The Commanding Heights, PBS, https://www.pbs.org/wgbh/commandingheights/shared/minitext/int_pchidambaram.

html. In an ironic twist, at time of writing Chidambaram is in jail on charges of corruption.

Chapter 13: George Orwell, Public Choice, and Doublethink

1. This chapter was inspired by George Mason University economist Bryan Caplan, "Orwell as Public Choice Socialist," Econlib, May 6, 2015, and by Michael Makovi, "George Orwell as a Public Choice Economist," *American Economist* 60, no. 2 (November 1, 2015): 183–208.

2. Josef Stalin, "Address to the 16th Congress of the Russian Communist Party," *Pravda* 177 (1930), https://www.marxists.org/reference/archive/stalin/works/1930/aug/27.htm.

Chapter 14: Has Real Socialism Never Been Tried?

1. Sunkara, *The Socialist Manifesto,* 153.

2. Ibid., 30.

3. Johan Norberg, "Bernie's Right: America Should Be More like Sweden, *Reason,* May 2016, https://reason.com/2016/04/18/bernies-rightamerica-should-be/.

4. In the Heritage Foundation's *Index of Economic Freedom 2020,* Sweden ranks as more free than the U.S.A. in six of twelve categories, and the U.S. more free than Sweden in four of the twelve (the other two are tied). Were it not for Sweden's large tax burden and government spending it would certainly rank as more free than the U.S. over all. See Terry Miller, Anthony Kim, and James M. Roberts, *2020 Index of Economic Freedom* (Washington, D.C.: Heritage Foundation, 2020), https://www.heritage.org/index/.

5. Carl Ratner, "False Consciousness," *Encyclopedia of Critical Psychology* (Spring 2013), http://www.sonic.net/~cr2/false%20consc.htm.

Chapter 15: But Isn't Inequality a Real Problem?

1. John Cassidy, "Why Socialism Is Back," *New Yorker*, June 18, 2019, https://www.newyorker.com/news/our-columnists/why-socialism-is-back.

2. Chris Giles, "Piketty Findings Undercut by Errors," *Financial Times*, May 23, 2014.

3. Chris Edwards and Ryan Bourne, "Exploring Wealth Inequality," Policy Analysis 881, Cato Institute, November 5, 2019, https://www.cato.org/publications/policy-analysis/exploring-wealth-inequality.

4. Gerald Auten and David Splinter, "Income Inequality in the United States: Using Tax Data to Measure Long-Term Trends," David Splinter, December 20, 2019, http://davidsplinter.com/AutenSplinter-Tax_Data_and_Inequality.pdf.

5. Matthew Smith, *et al.*, "Top Wealth in the United States: New Estimates and Implications for Taxing the Rich," Erik Zwick, July 19, 2019, http://ericzwick.com/wealth/wealth.pdf.

6. N. Gregory Mankiw, "Spreading the Wealth Around: Reflections Inspired by Joe the Plumber," *Eastern Economic Journal* 36 (2010): 285–98.

7. Fred Smith and Ryan Young, "Virtuous Capitalism: Why There Is Less Corruption in Business than You Think," Profiles in Capitalism No. 1, Competitive Enterprise Institute, October 2015.

8. Up to a cap.

9. This case is developed in detail by Randal O'Toole of the Cato Institute in *American Nightmare: How Government Undermines the Dream of Home Ownership* (Washington, D.C.: Cato Institute 2012).

10. Peter J. Wallison, *Hidden in Plain Sight: What Really Caused the World's Worst Financial Crisis—and Why It Could Happen Again* (New York: Encounter Books, 2016).

11. Michelle Minton, "The Community Reinvestment Act's Harmful Legacy," OnPoint 132, Competitive Enterprise Institute, March 2008, https://cei.org/sites/default/files/Michelle%20Minton%20-%20 CRA%20-%20FINAL_WEB.pdf.

Chapter 16: *Radical Equality and Doublethink*

1. Remember how Arnold Kling noted the "oppressor" groups were excluded from the language of social justice.
2. Yuka Hayashi, "Lawmakers Dispute Method to Identify Victims of Racial Bias in Auto Lending," *Wall Street Journal*, January 19, 2016.
3. For a good examination of this positive case, see Charles Murray, *In Our Hands* (Washington, D.C.: AEI Press, 2006).

Chapter 18: *The Individual and the Collective*

1. Douglas B. Rasmussen and Douglas J. Den Uyl, *Norms of Liberty: A Perfectionist Basis for Non-Perfectionist Politics* (University Park, Pennsylvania: Pennsylvania State University Press, 2005).
2. Sunkara, *The Socialist Manifesto.*

Chapter 19: *Positive and Negative Rights*

1. John Adams, *The Revolutionary Writings of John Adams, Selected and with a Foreword by C. Bradley Thompson* (Indianapolis, Indiana: Liberty Fund, 2000). Adams's "A Dissertation on the Canon and Feudal Law" was originally published in 1765.

Chapter 20: *Free Stuff, or Free People?*

1. List collated from The Labour Party, "It's Time for Real Change: The Labour Party Manifesto 2019," https://labour.org.uk/ wp-content/uploads/2019/11/Real-Change-Labour- Manifesto-2019.pdf.

2. Andrew Rawnsley, "Free Stuff for Absolutely Everyone. What Could Possibly Go Wrong with That?" *Observer*, November 17, 2019.
3. George Selgin, "The Nice Limits of Modern Monetary Theory," Alt-M blog, Cato Institute, May 10, 2019. https://www.alt-m.org/2019/05/10/the-nice-limits-of-modern-monetary-theory/.
4. This is one of economist David R. Henderson's "ten pillars of economic wisdom," laid out in his book *The Joy of Freedom*, which I commend to everyone. David R. Henderson, *The Joy of Freedom: An Economist's Odyssey* (Upper Saddle River, New Jersey: Prentice Hall Books, 2001).

Chapter 21: Alienation Nation
1. "Marxism & Alienation," Marxists, https://www.marxists.org/subject/alienation/index.htm.
2. Karl Marx, *Economic & Philosophic Manuscripts of 1844*, trans. Martin Milligan (Moscow: Progress Publishers, 1959).
3. Adam Smith, *An Inquiry into the Nature and Causes of the Wealth of Nations by Adam Smith, edited with an Introduction, Notes, Marginal Summary and an Enlarged Index by Edwin Cannan* (London: Methuen, 1904) 1, no. 178, originally published in 1776.
4. Deirdre McCloskey, *The Bourgeois Virtues: Ethics for an Age of Commerce* (Chicago: University of Chicago Press, 2007).
5. The classical virtues are courage, justice, prudence, and temperance, while the Christian virtues are faith, hope, and love.
6. Joseph A. Schumpeter, *Capitalism, Socialism, and Democracy* (New York: Harper & Row, 1962).

Chapter 22: Property Rights and Economic Freedom
1. Erica York, *et al.*, "Tax Freedom Day 2019 Is April 16th," Tax Foundation, April 10, 2019; The Adam Smith Institute, https://

www.adamsmith.org/taxfreedomday; Bund der Steuerzahler, "Von 1 Euro bleiben nur 47,6 Cent," July 9, 2015, http://www.genussmaenner.de/aid=39158.phtml; Cecile Philippe, "La pression sociale et fiscale réelle du salarié moyen au sein de l'UE — 9ème edition," Institut Economique Molinari, July 27, 2018, https://www.institutmolinari.org/2018/07/27/la-pression-sociale-et-fiscale-reelle-du-salarie-moyen-au-sein-de-lue-9eme-edition/.

2. James Gwartney, Robert Lawson, and Joshua Hall, *Economic Freedom of the World 2018* (Fraser Institute/Cato Institute, 2018), https://www.cato.org/economic-freedom-world.

3. Gonzalo Schwarz, "The Importance of Structural Factors in Understanding Economic Mobility," Archbridge Institute, October 4, 2018, https://www.archbridgeinstitute.org/2018/10/09/the-importance-of-structural-factors-in-understanding-economic-mobility/.

Chapter 23: Regulation, Not Calculation

1. "Senator Warren Urges Regulators and Companies to Increase Oversight, Address Health Impacts of E-Cigarette Products," Elizabeth Warren's Senate website, https://www.warren.senate.gov/newsroom/press-releases/senator-warren-urges-regulators-and-companies-to-increase-oversight-address-health-impacts-of-e-cigarette-products.

2. It is interesting to note that AOC has not jumped on this bandwagon. It may be that her experience as a bartender has suggested that a vaping crackdown may have unintended consequences.

Chapter 25: Free Speech and the Socialist Commonwealth

1. See, for example, Samuel Farber, "A Socialist Approach to Free Speech," *Jacobin*, https://www.jacobinmag.com/2017/02/garton-ash-free-speech-milo-yiannopoulos.

Chapter 26: Liberty for Its Own Sake—and for Our Health

1. Proudhon also proclaimed, "Property is freedom!" For him it was the theft (by capitalists) that was the problem, not the property. Towards the end of his life he wrote that "property is the only power that can act as a counterweight to the State." Proudhon was no capitalist, but he was also no Marxist.
2. "2019 Employer Health Benefits Survey," Kaiser Family Foundation, https://www.kff.org/health-costs/report/2019-employer-health-benefits-survey/.
3. "Testimony of Jim R. Purcell, Chairman, State National Bank of Big Spring, Big Spring, Texas, and Chairman Texas Bankers Association before the Committee on Financial Services U.S. House of Representatives July 12, 2016," https://financialservices.house.gov/uploadedfiles/07.12.2016_jim_purcell_testimony.pdf.

Chapter 28: Socialism and the Divine

1. See, for example, the language of the Massachusetts Body of Liberties, a constitution enacted in 1651: "If any man after legal conviction shall have or worship any other god, but the lord god, he shall be put to death."
2. Karl Marx, *Critique of Hegel's Philosophy of Right*, ed. Joseph O'Malley (Cambridge, Massachusetts: Cambridge University Press, 1970). First published in 1843.
3. Quoted in Samuel Gregg, "Reason, Faith, and the Struggle for Western Civilization," (Washington, D.C.: Regnery, 2019); V. I. Lenin, "Socialism and Religion," *Novaya Zhizn* 28, December 3,

1905, https://www.marxists.org/archive/lenin/works/1905/dec/03. htm.

4. This is not the place to go into Pope Francis' complicated relationship with liberation theology, but it is safe to say that he is much more sympathetic to its arguments than either of his two immediate predecessors, who strongly condemned the theology involved.

5. Andrew R. Lewis and Paul A. Djupe, "Americans May Be Too Religious to Embrace Socialism," FiveThirtyEight, March 10, 2016, https://fivethirtyeight.com/features/americans-may-be-too-religious-to-embrace-socialism/.

6. David French, "Liberty Gained and Power Lost," The Dispatch, January 10, 2020, https://thedispatch.com/p/liberty-gained-and-power-lost.

7. Michael Greve, *The Upside Down Constitution* (Cambridge, Massachusetts: Harvard University Press, 2012).

Chapter 29: *How Socialism Discourages Virtuous Behavior*

1. Marx, Karl, Friedrich Engels, Vladimir I. Lenin, and E. Czobel, *Critique of the Gotha Programme* (New York: International Publishers, 1970).

2. Nicholas Eberstadt, *Men without Work: America's Invisible Crisis* (West Conshohocken, Pennsylvania: Templeton Foundation Press, 2012).

3. Ibid., October 3, 2016.

4. This section was written before the massive explosion in unemployment caused by the COVID-19 crisis. See the Afterword for more.

5. Jarrett Skorup, "No Horses, but Detroit Water Department Employs 'Horseshoer,'" Michigan Capitol Confidential, August 2, 2012, https://www.michigancapitolconfidential.com/17404.

Chapter 30: Transnationalism and Nationalism

1. American translation by Charles Hope Kerr. The American version is explicit about the role of labor union, including the words, "Toilers from shops and fields united, / The union we of all who work: / The earth belongs to us, the workers, / No room here for the shirk." The British version, on the other hand, talks about soldiers mutinying and shooting their own generals.

2. John Fonte, "Liberal Democracy vs. Transnational Progressivism: The Future of the Ideological Civil War Within the West," *Orbis*, Summer 2002, https://www.ngo-monitor.org/data/images/File/transnational_progressivism_08312002.pdf.

3. Under the Constitution, the Senate does not actually ratify treaties. It provides advice and consent to the president to ratify them. In practice, this means that the Senate vote is the de facto if not de jure vote on ratification. It is possible that a Senate might consent to a treaty submitted by a president who then changes his mind.

Chapter 31: Watermelon Environmentalism

1. H.Res.109–Recognizing the duty of the Federal Government to create a Green New Deal, 116th Congress (2019–2020). Introduced February 7, 2019.

2. Richard Qiu, "How Singapore Is Retraining Workers for a More Automated Workplace," Axios, March 6, 2019, https://www.axios.com/how-singapore-is-retraining-workers-for-a-more-automated-workplace-0d31856b-39e5-4159-8a59-9b3ee02e7419.html.

3. John Russo and Sherry Lee Linkon, "Deindustrialization," ed. Richard McCormack, *Manufacturing a Better Future for America* (Alliance for American Manufacturing, 2009).

4. James Bovard, "The Folly of Federal Training," Foundation for Economic Education, April 26, 2012 , https://fee.org/articles/the-folly-of-federal-training/.

5. See, e.g., Marlo Lewis, "A Citizen's Guide to Climate Change," OnPoint 255, Competitive Enterprise Institute, June 11, 2019, https://cei.org/content/citizens-guide-climate-change?gclid=CjoK CQjwwr32BRD4ARIsAAJNf_1hWk2vAJPq3vTKZpHpGJySLCag VqkCm-srdIdJh-HBZiUkWesQ1LA aAtogEALw_wcB.

Chapter 33: Business and Civil Society

1. Alexis de Tocqueville, *Democracy In America* (New York: G. Dearborn & Co., 1838), Chapter 29.
2. Edward Shils, "The Virtue of Civil Society," *Government and Opposition* 26, no. 1 (Winter 1991).
3. Again, I am not including the early voluntarist socialists here.
4. Roland Boer, "What Is a Socialist Civil Society," Political Theology Network, May 28, 2016, https://politicaltheology.com/what-is-a-socialist-civil-society/.
5. Timothy P. Carney, *Alienated America: Why Some Places Thrive While Others Collapse* (New York: HarperCollins, 2019).
6. Eberstadt, *Men without Work*.
7. Carney, *Alienated America*.
8. Richard Morrison, "Review: 'Alienated America' by Timothy P. Carney," Competitive Enterprise Institute, April 5, 2019, https://cei.org/blog/review-alienated-america-timothy-p-carney.
9. Pun intended.

Chapter 35: Tocqueville's Warning

1. Dana Rose Falcone, "Jerry Seinfeld: College students don't know what the hell they're talking about," Entertainment Weekly, June 8, 2015.

2. Lukianoff, Greg, and Jonathan Haidt. *The Coddling of the American Mind: How Good Intentions and Bad Ideas Are Setting Up a Generation for Failure* (New York: Penguin Press, 2018).

Chapter 36: You Can't Beat Government with Government

1. There is no doubt at all that China has been a bad actor on trade and that something needs to be done about it. Tariffs, however, are the bluntest of instruments.
2. Quoted in Daniel Crane, "All I Really Know about Antitrust I Learned in 1912," *Iowa Law Review* 100, no. 2025 (2015), https://ilr.law.uiowa.edu/print/volume-100-issue-5/all-i-really-need-to-know-about-antitrust-i-learned-in-1912/.
3. "Corporate Accountability and Democracy," Bernie Sanders (campaign website, https://berniesanders.com/issues/corporate-accountability-and-democracy/?mod=article_inline.
4. Pun intended.

Chapter 37: America's Immunity to Socialism

1. Kathy Sawyer, "AFL-CIO Toils in Foreign Vineyards," *Washington Post*, November 19, 1983, https://www.washingtonpost.com/archive/politics/1983/11/19/afl-cio-toils-in-foreign-vineyards/7f4d3f11-00ed-49b3-a25e-aafcaa521dca/.
2. Fred Smith, "A New History of American Business," *Forbes*, September 8, 2015, https://www.forbes.com/sites/fredsmith/2015/09/04/a-new-history-of-american-business/#49e3b5a29e2d.
3. Frank S. Meyer, *"In Defense of Freedom" and Related Essays* (Indianapolis, Indiana: Liberty Fund, 1996).

Chapter 38: Is It Different This Time?

1. Herbert Marcuse, *Counterrevolution and Revolt*,(Boston: Beacon Press, 1972). Marcuse also advocated the promotion of "ecology,"

as environmentalism was then called, by using the "capitalist framework" against itself.

Chapter 40: Reagan's Challenge

1. Joanne Finnegan, "Poll Finds 49% of Doctors Support 'Medicare for All," Fierce Healthcare, May 30, 2019, https://www.fiercehealthcare.com/practices/poll-finds-49-doctors-support-medicare-for-all.

Chapter 41: The Powell Memorandum

1. Lewis F. Powell, "The Powell Memorandum: Attack on American Free Enterprise System," Powell Archives, Washington & Lee University School of Law, https://scholarlycommons.law.wlu.edu/powellmemo/.
2. Fred L. Smith Jr., "A New History of American Business," *Forbes*, September 8, 2015, https://www.forbes.com/sites/fredsmith/2015/09/04/a-new-history-of-american-business/#9a8b1119e2dd.
3. "The Lewis Powell Memo: A Corporate Blueprint to Dominate Democracy," Greenpeace USA, https://www.greenpeace.org/usa/democracy/the-lewis-powell-memo-a-corporate-blueprint-to-dominate-democracy/.

Chapter 42: Meeting Reagan's Challenge

1. Steven Horwitz, "Economics as the Study of Peaceful Human Cooperation and Progress," keynote address delivered on December 17, 2019 in Athens, Greece at the Center for Liberal Studies Annual Prometheus Awards Dinner.
2. Ronald Reagan, "What Ever Happened to Free Enterprise," Ludwig Von Mises Memorial Lecture at Hillsdale College, November 10, 1977.

Chapter 43: Heightening the Contradictions

1. Kristian Niemietz, *Socialism: The Failed Idea That Never Dies* (London: London Publishing, 2019), 18.

Index